Praise for *Standing O!*

"An uplifting read with tangible life lessons from a terrific group of leaders."
- ***Jared Augustine, CEO, Thuzio***

"What the world needs right now is positive energy and uplifting stories. Thank you to Scott for giving all of us a dose of badly needed unification."
- ***Steve Richard,* Founder *of ExecVision, Vorsight, & Funnel Clarity***

"We all need stories. They convey incredible messages and guidelines to test out in our own lives. *Standing O!* is a torrent of gems to help anyone gain some wisdom from many different voices. You are bound to find one if not many lessons to capture more motivation or knowledge."
- ***Brett Hughes, Philanthropist, Co-Founder of Lacrosse the Nations, Entrepreneur, Retired Professional Lacrosse player & NCAA National Lacrosse Champion at the University of Virginia***

"An amazingly timely book as the digital landscape continues to encourage attention seeking behavior. *Standing O!* is all about turning the spotlight on others. Great stories about lessons learned and the strength, fortitude and love people have received from their support systems. A book like this gives me gratitude and is a reminder of what makes America such a great place to live."
- ***Ben Thibeault, Enterprise Sales Manager, LinkedIn***

"*Standing O!* is a collection of amazing and inspiring stories that will help push you to succeed in your life or career. Once you start reading, you won't be able to stop."
- ***Jarrod Jordan, Global Chief Marketing Officer, Keynote Speaker***

"*Standing O!* gives a glimpse behind the curtain of exceptional people. It provides insight into what and who inspires greatness and fuels success. Their story, in their words about those that ultimately changed the lives of many. Leaders aren't born, they are crafted by circumstances. These stories tell us about the transformational inspiration behind the curtain. Wonderful concept and an extraordinary book."
- ***Michael Carr, Co-Founder of TeraComm & CEO of XSoptix***

grat-i-tude:
the quality of being thankful, readiness to show appreciation for and return kindness

"Gratitude makes sense of our past, brings peace for today, and creates vision for tomorrow."
-Melody Beattie

Standing O!

A collection of essays from successful people
about the role models who inspired them.

ISBN: 978-1-947486-07-2(paperback)

Eaton Press
EatonPress.com

Table of Contents

Dedicated to:

Meg MacGregor
SomethingNew and all of the good — including this book — that has come from it, would not have happened without your love and support. I love you!

Tucker & Cooper MacGregor
Two of the most resilient people on the planet. I believe in you and love you guys!

Foreword - Dick Vermeil

Dick Vermeil is a legendary football coach and broadcaster. He led the Philadelphia Eagles to the Super Bowl and the St. Louis Rams to their only Super Bowl victory. Vermeil owns the distinction of being named "Coach of the Year" on four levels: high school, junior college, NCAA Division 1 and professional football. In all three of his stints as an NFL head coach, Vermeil took each team—Philadelphia, St. Louis and the Kansas City Chiefs, each of which had a losing record before he arrived—and took them to the playoffs by his third season at the helm. He is enshrined in the Philadelphia Eagles Hall of Fame and the St. Louis Rams Ring of Honor.

....

Whenever I stop and seriously think about how many people have positively moved me through the different periods of my life, I think of the word "emulation." The older I get, the more I think about all the people who have, at one time or another, said something, done something, or suggested I think about something that shaped the paths I took through my career.

My best example: In my senior year (1954) in high school, a young first-year football coach came to Calistoga High School to teach history and coach football and track. This was Bill Wood's first job. He was very passionate about it, and his passion was easily read. Once we got going and were doing well, Coach Wood approached me after a practice session and said, "You know, Dick, if you wanted to, you could play college football."

His statement startled me in a positive way. I remember thinking, "Wow, that would be great if I really could do that." My whole attitude about the game changed. No one had ever told me I was really good at anything, and to hear Coach say that pumped me up big time. It was hard for me to believe I could play like those I watched on TV on Saturday afternoons. The other thing Coach said to me was, "By looking at your transcripts, you haven't been doing much in the way of academic preparation for college, so you'll have to go to a community college." In evaluating his statement, I knew he was right because I had planned to go into business with my dad in his garage: Vermeil and Sons. I had already started working in the shop the day after grammar school graduation.

With Coach's push, I decided to go to Napa Junior College that fall, play football, catch up academically, and then see if his evaluation was correct. Along with his push, he also injected his passion for the game. I was becoming more than just a young kid learning to play quarterback. I was really getting into the Xs and Os of the game, especially on the offensive side, and had a hard time concentrating on anything else. It didn't take me long to become a know-it-all. I probably drove my junior college coach crazy with all the ideas and suggestions I had to offer that, in my opinion, were better than his.

Many years have passed since Bill Wood's positive influence on my life's path, but what he passed on to me has forever been engrained in my mind. In fact, it became the foundation of my coaching philosophy, which went on to achieve a World Championship Super Bowl ring. My thinking was and still is: If his positive reinforcement, his caring, and great example could influence me at a young age, why wouldn't it work for the kids I'm going to coach now?

Consequently, I continued to build on his foundation over my next thirty-five years of coaching. I built on it, refined it, added to it, and learned from it, but I never really changed his foundation.

1. Let your players know you care about them. This is true at all levels of coaching.
2. Make sure they see in you all the traits you want to see in them. Be a good example that is worthy of emulation.
3. Create a positive atmosphere in which you coach them, an atmosphere that will help them believe in themselves and enjoy becoming the best they can be.
4. Define your plan and make it clear how they fit into it. Define your vision for them, your value system, your purpose, and your process.
5. Teach them that hard work and fatigue are not forms of punishment. They are solutions, problem solvers, and improvement tools that

must be in place and understood if your players are going to be the best they can be.

6. Build relationships as you implement your vision, values, and process. When you have a great relationship with your players, they will give you permission to lead them.
7. Be sincere, always tell the truth, and be honest. There is no way you can lead a person or a team of people if you haven't established credibility with them, and the only way you can do this is by being honest and trustworthy.

Winning is not complicated. People complicate it by not seeking people worthy of emulation. I've been exposed to so many emulators that to write about each would be a book in itself, but let these lessons I shared be a good example for you to appreciate your emulators.

Be grateful because very few of us did what we've done based on our own brilliance.

Dick Vermeil

Scott MacGregor - Introduction

Scott MacGregor is the founder & CEO of SomethingNew LLC, one of the fastest growing talent acquisition companies in the country, and a three-time recipient of the American Business Award for Innovation. MacGregor's belief that good companies do good things led him to establish SomethingGood™, which is the social mission component of SomethingNew. Standing O! *is part of that mission as all of the proceeds are going to Keep on Playing and Elevate New York, where MacGregor currently serves as board chair.*

....

My goals in putting together *Standing O!* (which Meredith Maslich, CEO at Eaton Press, informed me is an anthology, I had no clue) were:

1. Give a wide audience the opportunity to learn important life lessons from people who have impacted my life.
2. Give the authors of the essays the opportunity to express gratitude to the people who influenced them.
3. Raise awareness and money for two great organizations: Keep on Playing and Elevate New York.

Life is cumulative, and my life has been enriched by more people than I could ever mention. There are, however, some people whose impact has been the most profound — I'll call them "The Great Eight"— and like this book's contributing authors, they are an eclectic mix of people with a common denominator. These eight inspiring mentors invested in me, and believed in me, and they are some of the most resilient, passionate, hardworking people I've ever met.

First is my Uncle Ray, whom I adopted as my Grandfather, because both of my grandfathers passed away before I was born. When Uncle Ray passed away he was buried with the homemade certificate we had made to "officially" adopt him as my Grandfather. Ray Jopson was the smartest person I knew and also the humblest. I spent hours talking to him at his kitchen table, soaking up his Encyclopedic knowledge. There was no subject he could not converse fluently in. He was a master craftsman with a magical and immaculate workshop where, with meticulous attention to detail, he made some of the things that became my most prized possessions. These were gifts of love that took countless hours to build.

He worked for decades for the *Shoreline Times,* always keeping his job as a linotype setter even when he had quietly and inconspicuously become one of the owners of the paper. He always put others before him. He devoted his life to taking care of his parents and then married the love of his life, my Aunt Franny. She was a constant positive force in my life, always excited to see me, and number two on my Great Eight list. When my aunt died unexpectedly, Uncle Ray changed dramatically, and I always believed it was from a broken heart. After he passed away, I was cleaning out his house and found a box on a closet shelf. Inside were dozens of neatly cut-out newspaper clippings from my days in Little League through my high school career. To my Uncle/Grandfather Ray and my Aunt Franny, I want to give you both a standing O for teaching me humility and what a true servant's mentality looks like.

My best friend from Kindergarten to the present is Dave Green. A football teammate and truly someone who has been there for me my entire life. His father, Ken Green, is the third of the "Great Eight." I grew up poor in Madison, Connecticut, an affluent shoreline town, where everyone seemed rich and successful. I saw my parents struggle financially and never wanted that stress for myself and my own family. Ken Green was a successful businessman and someone I admired for his intelligence, dedication, and professionalism. He was the Vice President of a medical supply company, and I watched him travel the country and treat his craft with a level of professionalism that made me see a career in sales as admirable.

Ken or "Papa Green," as I often called him, was always learning, reading, playing guitar, writing songs, performing, running, playing tennis or swimming. He was also interested in my education, was proud of me when I made Honor Roll and always asked me about what became a voracious reading habit. When I graduated from college, he gave me a generous graduation gift to buy my first suit for my new career in sales, and even more important to me, a card expressing his belief in me and my future. Throughout the years, despite living on opposite coasts we still talk from time to time and he never fails to tell me how proud he is of me. Papa Green I want to give you a standing O for teaching me what professionalism looks like.

Coaches can play a huge role in shaping someone's life. I had the incredible good fortune to play for two Hall of Fame coaches during my high school athletic career. Coach Larry Ciotti is a legend. He began a program at Daniel Hand High School in Madison, Connecticut, in 1970, and over the course of the next eighteen years, he won five state championships while amassing a 141-41-2 record and leading a team in my freshman year that was the first ever from the state of Connecticut to be ranked in the USA Today Top 25. In 2011 Coach Ciotti was awarded the Walter Camp Football Foundation Lifetime Achievement Award. Following his career at Hand, he coached for another twenty-one years at Yale University. I know I'm not alone when I say that, to this day Coach Ciotti still scares me a little.

While Coach Ciotti was my head coach, my position coach in football was Steve Filippone, who also doubled as my baseball coach. Let me just say that Coach Filippone coached baseball like he coached football. Intense doesn't begin to describe it. Following a legend is never easy, but from 1989 to 2016 he was able to win seven State Championships while compiling a 223-82-5 record. Coach Filippone was also inducted into the Hall of Fame and was the 2013 National High School Athletic Association Coach of the Year.

The program's unprecedented success came from the hard work, discipline, and pride instilled by these two exceptional coaches. They pushed us way past what we thought was our breaking point and excuses were never allowed, only excellence. My business success has never been because I am the smartest or most talented. Any success I have had, has come from tenacity, hard work, passion, dedication, discipline and resiliency — all traits honed by these inspirational coaches. And are all reasons why Coach Larry Ciotti and Coach Steve Filippone take slots four and five on my list and deserve a standing O.

Some people have tragedy strike and lead a tragic life, while others have tragedy strike and keep on going and make the world a better place. My Aunt Betty Mulvey is the second kind of person and is number six on my list. When I was very young, I remember her husband, my Uncle Joe, dying of cancer and leaving behind a single mother to raise five children. Over the years, two of her daughters suffered horrific accidents, years apart, that left each of them in a coma. Despite even more heartache, my Aunt Betty has remained perpetually upbeat. Her glass is always more than half full and her focus is always on others. For teaching me about untold resiliency and never being a victim, a big standing O to my Aunt Betty.

Last, but certainly not least, are my two grandmothers: Ethel MacGregor and May Traub (two names that I think have been retired in their honor). Both were forces of nature, both were tough as nails and both lived life to the fullest and made everyone they met better because they knew them. My grandmother Traub was born in 1900 and my grandmother MacGregor in 1911, and both lived into their nineties, strong and independent to the end. My grandmothers were amazing women who never and I mean never—complained. Their work ethic and energy were legendary. One was a teacher and church leader who was active politically, and the other was a farmer, accomplished cook (for Walt Disney, Supreme Court Justices, and for many years, the Headmaster of Choate Rosemary Hall), seamstress, and maker of dandelion wine. Both were avid supporters of everything I did and invested a ton of time in me despite being extremely busy. Bright and fiercely independent, they set the pace for us all in how to live with no regrets and with passion.

I have been blessed with an amazing life, and I owe it all to the lessons I learned from Ray Jopson, Franny Jopson, Ken Green, Larry Ciotti, Steve Filippone, Betty Mulvey, Ethel MacGregor and May Traub, and so many others who continue to inspire me today.

And now I'm excited to share with you this collection of additional standing O's, submitted by our contributors. The authors and subjects of these essays are a combination of names known and unknown but each story is inspirational and filled with important life lessons.

I cannot say an adequate thank you to the amazing contributing authors in this anthology. Their life stories remind me that anything is possible, and I'm proud and grateful to call them friends.

I hope that as you read through this book you will take a minute and think about who in your own life deserves a standing O and then share it with them.

Enjoy!

Scott MacGregor, CEO
SomethingNew LLC

Michaela Alexis

Michaela Alexis is an entrepreneur from Ottawa, Canada. In 2016, her article about landing her dream job went viral on LinkedIn. She has since replicated her viral success with multiple articles, photo and video campaigns, with articles featured on CNBC, Success.com, Buzzfeed, and more. Armed with just a tiny dry-erase board and writing skills, she has built a mega presence on LinkedIn tackling tough business conversations.

....

Lately, I've been all about minimalism. Sure, I still collect an embarrassing number of sassy mugs and have a weak spot for hardcover biographies and travel memoirs, but I've found that life is lovelier with less in my home.

On one of my recent decluttering sprees, I started tossing out old birthday and wedding congratulations cards. I grazed my thumb across one at the bottom of the pile. It was nothing special, just a typical card you pick up at the last minute from your local pharmacy with a glittery font sprawled across the cover and a generic message about enjoying the year ahead.

Then I reread the handwritten message: "I'm so proud of you. Just remember…we must make the path by walking (or, some of us, by running!). There's so much ahead for you. Just take it one step at a time."

It was a card that my mom had given me right before my life and career were transformed.

I had just been laid off, and despite my own insecurities about my future, she always saw the twinkle of potential in me. Her faith in my ability to persevere has always been unwavering throughout the seasons of my life.

The first thing that comes to mind whenever I think of my mom and the impact that she's had on my life is a footprint.

My mom was the one who clasped my chubby palm as I took my first few steps as a baby.

My mom was the one who taught me how to sprint when she nudged me out the front door and told me to run to catch the school bus.

My mom was the one who cultivated a love of travel and experiences in me, allowing me to dip my toes in salty waves, chase seagulls across sandy beaches, and march along wild trails full of history and wonder.

My mom was the one who tolerated my dramatic, stomping escapes from home, knowing full well that I'd just end up sitting on the curb until dusk. All it took was the smell of her warm lasagna wafting into the summer air to drag my appetite and ego back inside.

When I developed agoraphobia and struggled to take steps outside, my mom sat with me in that pain, without judgment or shame.

My mom was the one who, after her heartbreaking split from my dad, decided to reclaim her life instead of wallowing in sorrow. She returned to track and field—a sport that she's been passionate about since she was little—at a time when most people are thinking about retirement.

Watching her erupt from the starting blocks and sprint toward the finish line has taught me that when the blueprint of your life is set ablaze, you still have a choice. You get to decide how to react. You can lie down and wait for the clock to run out, or you can tie on some sneakers and continue to chase (sometimes literally) your dreams.

Two years ago, my confident strut became a sluggish crawl. I was lost, broke, and afraid that my whole life was destined to be failures and disappointments on repeat. It was my mom who took a deep breath and reminded me of the thing that she's reminded me of my whole life—that simple truth that we often lose sight of when we become so consumed with how our story will end.

Just take that first step.

Mark Allen

Mark Allen has been acknowledged by ESPN as the greatest endurance athlete of all time. He is the six-time Ironman Triathlon World Champion and was named triathlete of the year six times by Triathlete *magazine.* Outside *magazine dubbed him the worlds fittest man in 1997, the same year Allen was inducted into the Ironman Hall of Fame. He was also inducted into the USA Triathlon Hall of Fame and the International Triathlon Union Hall of Fame. He is the Founder of Mark Allen Coaching, LLC, author of* The Art of Competition, *and co-author with Brant Secunda of* Fit Soul, Fit Body: 9 Keys to a Healthier, Happier You.

....

My standing O goes to an unlikely person for a sportsman to choose as the human being who has had the most impact on his life. That great man is shaman and healer Brant Secunda.

Brant was trained in Mexico by the great shaman Don José Matsuwa. He taught Brant the Huichol tradition, which is an ancient system of health and healing that has been passed down from generation to generation for thousands of years.

I first met Brant at the halfway point of my triathlon career and began to study this beautiful tradition with him. To this day, his impact on my life has been broad and deep. Perhaps the best way to explain just a small sliver of that would be to share some of the simple but powerful life philosophy that Brant teaches. And I'd like to highlight that through a story from my final Ironman World Championship in 1995.

For those of you who are unfamiliar with the Hawaiian Ironman, here are the distances: It starts with a 2.4-mile ocean swim. That's followed by a 112-mile bike ride on a road that passes through hot, windy, desolate lava. The day is capped off with a marathon—26.2 miles of running. The fastest in the world cover this grueling distance in just over eight hours.

A great race starts with the training. Prepping for my final Ironman would mean logging about 15,000 miles of swimming, cycling, and running. Some days would go great. Others would be so far below where I needed to be that it would have been easy to give up. On those days, two things that Brant emphasized in his teachings would keep me on track. He underlined how important being humble was in Huichol life. That was a call to always continue on even if life didn't seem to be following our ideal plan.

He also taught that life can be a mystery and we might never know why things evolve as they do, but we should always trust that it is unfolding perfectly. On less-than-perfect days, I took solace in those two powerful thoughts, knowing that the tough days were just as important to have as the ones that went well. In the end, Brant helped me see that they were life's way of teaching me how to keep going even if things were not looking the way I had hoped.

I knew going into the race in 1995 that it would be my last. I'd won five straight Ironman World Championship titles in five starts already thanks to Brant's guidance. I was hoping to close out my career with a sixth and final victory.

I was tackling goals that no one had ever been able to accomplish in the history of the race. I was trying to win six Ironman titles in six starts, and I was trying to win as a thirty-seven-year-old. Neither of those had been done.

Unfortunately, I started the third and final portion of the race in fifth place. I was over thirteen minutes behind the leader, who was a twenty-four-year-old German soldier named Thomas Hellriegel. No one had ever come from that far down at the beginning of the marathon to be the champion. Now a third challenge was weighing heavily on my goals for the day.

All I could see was impossibility. The gap seemed way too big to close. About two miles into the marathon, I was ready to quit. I started having a quarrel within myself that turned into a raging battle. My mind was going crazy with all the chatter that was in no way helping me. "I want to quit. It's not worth it. I can't do it. But I can't just quit. I have to keep going. Just preserve your dignity and don't give up. But there's no hope. I don't like this. I don't need this!" Everyone has had those kinds of internal conversations at some point during life's challenges.

Brant had done many, many things to help me be ready for the race. But in that critical moment, it was the Huichol sayings that kept me going. He had told me again and again at his retreats that "it's not over until it's over. Just keep putting one foot in front of the other. From one moment to the next, something can shift."

Those precious words came back to me in that desperate moment early in the marathon. I was a step away from giving up and quitting. "Put one foot in front of the other." That was certainly not a call to give up and quit if things got tough.

Brant's words fortified me with the strength to keep going. But the battle raging in my head was still shackling my ability to fully engage in the race. There was no solution. I had come to win, but that was impossible. My sole purpose had been stripped away from me. The reins on the champion's chariot were squarely in the hands of another athlete leading the race thirteen minutes ahead of me.

Then a second aspect of Huichol culture that Brant stressed over and over came back to me. He'd say, "Stop the internal chatter. How can you hear life whispering to you with all that noise going on in your head? Just be quiet. Calm your mind and pay attention."

I had to find that quiet. I knew that unless I stopped the chatter my day would be a loss. My internal yelling was making it impossible to pay attention to the race. I was distracted from my best effort. Finally, I let it all go. My mind went quiet. Suddenly, I knew my purpose. It wasn't to win; it was to finish the best I could.

The whole race shifted. I stopped struggling with the impossible position I was in and embraced the idea to give the best effort I could. It took twenty-three miles of running, but eventually I did catch Hellriegel and went on to win my sixth and final Ironman World Championship title.

Huichol philosophy has helped me through all my life's challenges. On that particular day in 1995, it just happened that the challenge was on a racecourse. The impact was dramatic, as it has always been in helping me navigate the road bumps that come along the way in life. Not every situation turns out the way my ideal view would have it. But with Brant's help and his words, I've never given up in hopelessness.

Thank you, Brant. My standing O is for all you have done and continue to do to help me on my journey through life.

Max Altschuler

Max Altschuler is CEO of Sales Hacker Inc., the leading resource for modern business-to-business sales professionals. He's also the bestselling author of the books Hacking Sales *and* Career Hacking for Millennials. *He is an investor or advisor to more than fifty hyper-growth companies and a thought leader who's been featured in the* Harvard Business Review, Forbes, Inc., Time, *and many other publications.*

....

I might be in the minority because I know many will give their debt of gratitude to their mom or a coach. I'm giving my standing O to the pioneers of TV infomercials. One of the most useful lessons I ever learned was from watching infomercials as a kid. Although I loved watching people cook salivating and delicious meals, they actually ended up teaching me more than a few things I still use today.

Most infomercials have 30 minutes to wow buyers. They can't ask questions, so they prepare with tons of market research to predict what the viewer is likely to think and want to hear next. Watching QVC or "As Seen on TV" commercials has taught me more about buyer behavior than any book or college class.

One of my favorites is a 28-minute Ronco video pushing a Showtime Rotisserie and BBQ. You can find it on YouTube. It provides a perfect blueprint for things to hit on when creating any kind of marketing—whether a product pitch or a résumé. It includes:

1. Social proof. Great marketing includes third-party reviews from respected publications such as *Time* and *Forbes*. This infomercial has that, then later includes professional chefs, heart doctors, chicken farmers, and even audience members of different ages, genders, and

languages. It sends the message that experts recommend this. Apply this same idea to building your career by getting lots of recommendations and endorsements, and by getting colleagues to support you.

2. Targeted buyer segments. Buyers with similar profiles to target consumers are shown liking and appreciating the product. In the infomercial, you see a trendy dieter, hardcore foodie, coupon cutter, and busy parent. Words from someone who comes across as being like you are powerful in influencing purchase decisions. In your career, get references from people who match all sorts of profiles and share those references with people in similar positions when you want something.

3. Convenience. To sell, always make clear that whatever you're offering is easy to use and saves time. (Remember: Time is money—or even more precious than money.)

4. Durability. Whatever you've got, show that it's strong enough to last. In this infomercial, we actually see someone use a hammer, ostensibly to try to break the device. In your career, it can mean showing that your idea for a business is proven to make a long-lasting impact.

5. Broader good. It helps sway people to show them that they would not only be saving money but also doing something for the broader good. This infomercial says the rotisserie leads you to use less power, so your electric bills drop and you can help save the Earth. In your career, show how hiring you, promoting you, or letting you run a project would lead not only to profits and cost savings, but also a chance to advance your company's values. (These are often in brand statements or corporate statements of purpose.)

6. Style. The infomercial makes the device look great, and the company offers it in multiple colors to fit your kitchen. Whatever you're offering, always make it look its best. People respond to aesthetics. At Apple, Steve Jobs was obsessed with minute details of design. For you, this can mean dressing for the job you want or coming across in other ways—through social profiles and more—as fitting right in

with the style of that job.

7. Multiplying sales. When the opportunity is ripe, expand your sales. This infomercial encourages you to buy one for yourself and buy more for friends. In your career, if you spot an opportunity, encourage your boss to give you even more opportunities, resources, or time for learning.

8. Upsells. You also expand your sales by offering higher levels or add-ons. Ronco pushes skewers and other implements to make the product even more useful. In your career, this principle could mean telling potential funders for your idea that if they invest more, they stand to gain more.

9. Clever pricing models. Rather than selling the product for $100, the company offers "five easy payments of just $19.99." The use of multiple smaller payments helps convince people to buy. And, yes, all those nines instead of whole numbers help do the trick. They've been called charm prices or the left-digit effect. Because we read the left-most digit first, people psychologically feel more comfortable with the purchase. In your career, this can mean, for example, offering to start at a lower salary with scheduled increases over time.

10. Payment options. Offering many ways to pay helps. The infomercial lets people use credit or pay straight from their bank accounts. As you build your career, particularly when you do freelance or consulting work, giving people many convenient ways to pay you can make a big difference.

11. Guarantees. Offering money-back guarantees can be a big help in selling. They "evoke a positive emotional response, thereby increasing consumers' purchase intentions and willingness to pay a price premium," three researchers reported in the *Journal of Retailing*. Think about applying this to your own career by saying something like, "If I don't do a fantastic job for you, we can always part ways. But I will."

12. Scarcity and urgency. The infomercial drills in the idea that the deal being offered won't last long. How many times have you heard something like "while supplies last" or "you'd better act now!" These tactics work, with help from FOMO—the natural psychological fear of missing out. In your career, it can always be helpful to make clear that you have multiple opportunities, hear frequently from headhunters and are considering other options.

13. Memorability. You want people to remember what you offered. The more you do that, the more likely they are to eventually buy. The Ronco infomercial, like most product advertisements, uses a tagline designed to stick in your head. This same idea applies to marketing yourself through your résumé and interviews. Managers who remember you and think of you positively are more likely to hire you.

14. Repetition. Repeating key points can drive home a message and boost sales. There's a so-called Law of Seven, which suggests that people need to hear something seven times before they take action. It's also known as effective frequency. But it can lead to fatigue, making the consumer or hiring manager never want to hear about what you're offering ever again. So be careful not to overdo it.

15. Clear call to action. "Call to order now!" The infomercial pushes you to buy—and buy now, with no meetings or next steps necessary.

They know their audience and they've researched this sales process to a T. This is buying psychology at its finest. Who says you can't learn anything from watching too much TV?

Dave Anderson

Dave Anderson is the co-author of the bestseller Becoming a Leader of Character: 6 Habits That Make or Break a Leader at Work and at Home. *A second-generation West Point graduate, he earned a Bronze Star during Operation Desert Storm. While at a multinational Fortune 50 company, he earned the highest sales leadership award four times in eight years, and has written more than 500 articles on leadership and personal growth on his website: www.alslead.com.*

....

The boy's early story could rival that of Oliver Twist. At a young age, his mother dies and his alcoholic father abandons all the children at the county orphanage in a small Ohio coal town during the Great Depression. After a few years, his missing father returns to take some of his kids to a new home with a new wife. The boy is one of the lucky ones his father chooses. But six months later, the father sends the boy back to the orphanage for good.

For some people, that would be all the excuse they'd need to quit on themselves and on life. But that is not this boy's story. This boy's name is Jim.

By his senior year in high school, Jim was the captain of the football team and number one in his class. But children from the county orphanage did not go to college. Most went to work in the mines. Like them, Jim did not have the money to cover the costs of college. He decided the only way to get to college was the United States Military Academy at West Point.

Jim loved West Point. At the orphanage, he slept in a dormitory-style room with all the other boys. But at West Point, he only had two roommates at a time! He tried football. But the coach of the freshman football team, Vince Lombardi, informed him that he should try another sport.

Jim played lacrosse instead. He graduated on June 6, 1956, and married his high school sweetheart that same day.

Jim was the honor graduate of his Ranger School class and later a Ranger School instructor. As a counter-insurgency expert, he became an early advisor to the South Vietnamese army in 1963. He returned to Vietnam in 1969 as the aide-de-camp to General Creighton Abrams, the commanding general in South Vietnam. In 1970, he became the battalion commander for 1/5 Air Cavalry, 1st Cavalry Division.

In 1973, Jim became the Master of the Sword, the title given to the head of the Physical Education Department at West Point. He spent the next twenty-four years focused on the development of leaders of character at our nation's leadership school. On the day he retired, Jim was promoted to brigadier general.

At age eighty-two, Jim co-authored the Amazon bestseller *Becoming a Leader of Character: 6 Habits That Make or Break a Leader at Work and at Home.* Describing Jim's life based on those habits of character might be the best way to share why he deserves a standing O.

Courage: *Acting despite perceived or actual risk.*

Jim served two tours in Vietnam and earned the Silver Star, two Bronze Stars for valor, and a Purple Heart. Some of his combat experience was portrayed on the History channel's *Vietnam in HD.*

Humility: *Believing and acting like "It's not about me."*

Jim consistently deflects praise and gives credit to the officers and soldiers he was honored to lead throughout his forty-one-year Army career.

Integrity: *Doing what is good, right, and proper even at personal cost.*

Jim planned for and supported the admission of women to West Point in 1976, angering many of his contemporaries and superior officers. While he was Master of the Sword, over 2,000 women graduated from West Point. Many of those women are now general officers themselves.

Selflessness: *Putting the needs of others before our own needs, desires, and convenience.*

Jim chose to be the Master of the Sword even though the chief of staff of the Army at the time told him he was killing his chance for multiple generals' stars. Why? By going to West Point, he gave up the fast track, but his children gained time with their father.

Duty: *Acting based on my assigned tasks and moral obligations.*

Although retiring in his fifties would have meant fifteen years of lucrative corporate leadership jobs and retirement packages that dwarfed his military pension, Jim chose to stay at West Point to develop our nation's future leaders until his mandatory retirement age of sixty-four.

Positivity: *Displaying a positive and/or "can do" attitude in all circumstances.*

After retirement, Jim led his church congregation in a campaign to build an orphanage in Brazil, and two Sundays a month, he is the lead cook at the local soup kitchen because Jim truly believes everyone matters.

Courage, humility, integrity, selflessness, duty, and positivity are six habits of character General (Ret.) James L. Anderson, Ph.D., chose instead of succumbing to the easier path many young men in his situation might have chosen.

Because of him, I am now a professional speaker, consultant, and trainer who uses those six habits of character as the foundation for my message to leaders everywhere. He has handed the character message baton off to me to carry into the future.

The General, as he was called in the book, would tell you that everything in his past made him the man he is today. He is the best man I know and best exemplifies those habits of character we should all try to emulate. He is the man who gets my standing O. I am just blessed to call him Dad.

Alina Baikova

Alina Baikova is an international fashion model and founder of the mobile app Alina's Flowers. She has been featured in Vogue Ukraine, Australian Vogue, Spanish Harper's Bazaar, Elle, Grazia France, *and more.*

Sometimes I have days when I wake up and ask myself: What am I doing with my life? I'm thirty years old, and I have nothing. I'm not as successful as I want to be. I'm not married, and I have no kids and no business than will give me security in the future.

But then I look back to where I came from. Did I ever dream of the life I live now?

I came from a very small town in Ukraine called Kirovograd. You might not even find this city on a map. I have the best family, but none of my family members finished university. Everyone worked hard, but we were working class.

My mom gave birth to me when she was eighteen years old. My father used to cheat on her and even came to the delivery room with a mistress. They divorced when I was six and my sister was three. I never saw him until I started traveling when I was sixteen, and I had to have my father's permission to leave the country.

My mom used to work two jobs to take care of my sister and me. We moved into my grandmother's small apartment. In many countries, it was illegal to have so many people living in such a small space, but we didn't know any better. My mom became a heavy drinker. Now I understand how hard it was for her to go through all this when she was so young herself, but back then, I was ashamed, even though she would always make sure we had food and went to school. After she got divorced, she married the man I call my father. They were great partners. He helped her raise two kids, and when I was about seventeen, she went through alcohol hypnotherapy and never drank again.

Now I know so many people from different industries, and when I meet successful families, I can admit to myself how hard my childhood was. I used to think my mom didn't like bananas, but later I found out that she only had enough money to buy two bananas for me and my sister on special holidays a couple of times a year. I grew up seeing nothing and knowing nothing. I had never traveled to the ocean or the mountains, even though we have it all in Ukraine. When my high school English teacher told me I needed to focus on learning the English language, which I didn't care about, I would always say: "I have no chance to go to see the capital city in Ukraine. For sure I will never be able to travel where I need to speak English." I couldn't even dream of a bigger picture.

When I finished high school, instead of continuing my studies, I got a job as a waitress in a restaurant where I worked for twenty-four hours, followed by forty-eight hours off. My monthly salary was 10 euros a month plus tips. I went to work at sixteen because I didn't want to ask my family for money, and my mom was already working so hard.

We were having clothes made so all the waiters would be dressed the same, and one day when we went to a fitting, the woman from the dress shop asked me to walk for her. I found it odd that she had chosen me out of the whole group. So I walked, and she asked me if I was a model. I said no and added that I wasn't interested in being a model. In addition to the dress shop, she had a modeling agency. She gave me her card in case I changed my mind.

I was very tall and skinny, which made me insecure about my looks because at the time the fashion model look was Pamela Anderson. So I didn't believe I could be a model. Also, the fashion industry in Ukraine had a reputation for prostitution. I grew up watching TV programs about how girls traveled for modeling and were sold into prostitution. So nobody in my family would trust it.

After some time, I went to a club with my sister and a girl came up to me and asked if I was a model. She was very beautiful and told me a bit about modeling and her trips to China and invited me to come with her to a modeling agency to see if I might like it. It was the agency owned by the woman at the dress shop. I believe in destiny, and if something happens to you twice, you have to give it a chance.

So I went with her, and a month later, I was on a plane to China, where I made my first $1,000. It was such a big deal for me. I'm still in touch with the woman, Tatiana Ivanovna, and will be thankful to her for the rest of my life for believing in me and giving me the push I needed because she worked hard to convince me and my family to take a chance on this opportunity.

After the China trip, she put me on a bus with a bunch of beautiful girls and sent us to Kiev, Ukraine's capital, to visit a big agency. I still think all the other girls were prettier than me, but the agency chose me. I think it was luck and destiny.

I went to Moscow, where I did a couple of shows and had dinner with my agent and others. One of the other agents, Gia, told me: "You'll be big. You are the next Vodianova."

We applied for visas to travel to Milan, Paris, and New York, but I was only granted a visa to New York. The capital of fashion to me was Paris, so I didn't trust Gia and said I wouldn't go to New York. I was so afraid about being sold into prostitution and being too far from home for my family to help. But Gia passed away that year, and I found out he really was one of the best model scouts at the time. I regret my decision now because I missed at least five years of a great career. But I learned that everything happens for a reason, and there is a time for all when it's right.

The Kiev agency and Masha Manyuk from my original agency invited me to a casting call for a French modeling agency. And again from all the most beautiful girls, they chose me. I went to Paris for a couple of years and barely survived as a model, doing little jobs and living on pocket money. It was so hard, but I told myself that I wouldn't give up. The clients and agency would try to find problems with me: "You are too beautiful. You're too tall, too skinny, not open enough, or too open with people. You don't dress correctly. You should lie about your age."

I listened to everything and tried to change myself. I became even more insecure. I was lost. Then I understood that nothing was wrong with me. People have different tastes, and you can't be liked by everyone. So I stopped listening to what everyone was telling me and started focusing only on clients who were into my beauty. I became myself.

I had learned so much about fashion by then that I decided to find an agency in New York. I was twenty-four, which is late for models to start over with a new agency, but I went to the best one— Next Model Management. I had a meeting and told them: "I know I can do better. I know I can work a lot. I just need someone behind me who believes in me as much as I believe in myself."

They agreed to represent me but asked me to change my agencies worldwide. I immediately said yes and moved to New York. That's when my career really took off. I started making good money and felt that I should give something back, so I started helping a school for orphans back in my hometown and got involved with other charities. I'm a main ambassador of the Heart Fund, whose volunteers travel to developing countries to operate on children who have cardiovascular disease.

I have had a long, hard but very interesting journey to success. I never gave up even when I had the worst days of my life. I always believed in myself, and I have always been true to myself and the people around me. It wasn't easy, but I'm proud of myself and the choices I've made, and I'm grateful for the destiny that has brought me to where I am now. The people I surround myself with are those from whom I learn the most. They are the ones who challenge me and teach me.

Two things are the most important in life: family (because they will be there for you when you're successful and when you're down) and time. Spend your time wisely by always educating yourself and striving to be better than you were yesterday. Love the people around you, and help when someone needs help. Our lives are written for us. It always will be the way it has to be. Live, study, work hard, and see where life will take you.

John Barrows

John Barrows provides sales training and consulting services to some of the world's fastest-growing companies like Salesforce.com, LinkedIn, and Google. His experience spans all aspects of sales, from making 400 cold calls a week as an inside sales rep to serving as vice president of sales at his first startup, which was later sold to Staples. His main goal is to improve the overall education and quality of sales by sharing ideas and techniques that work.

....

I was born a "happy surprise" nine years after my sister. Now that I have a seven-year-old daughter, I know that no one in their right mind would plan to have another kid nine years after the first one. With that said, my parents didn't skip a beat and wanted to ensure I was given the same love and attention that my sister got, which is why I'm writing this standing O for them. Without their support and guidance from the start, there is no way I would be where I am today.

When my sister was born, my mom stayed home to care for her while my dad went to work. She eventually went back to work and got a great job at Wang Laboratories, one of the hottest companies in the country at the time. When I was born, she had to decide whether to stay at her job and get someone else to take care of me or quit and stay home. She made the decision to quit the job most people were fighting for and stay home with me so I could have the same experience and support that my sister had.

She didn't just stay home, though; eventually she started her own consulting practice out of our house and became a career counselor who helped people find work. I remember our living room was half living room and half office. We were the first family to have a copy machine in our house, which was kind of a big deal back then. My dad eventually became a consultant for the Federal Aviation Administration and worked out of his own home office. Even though I didn't know it at the time, they both exposed me to the world of entrepreneurship at a very early age before anyone even knew what it was.

In addition to being exposed to entrepreneurship, they exposed me to a lot more that helped shape me into the person I am today. My dad was a mechanical engineer with a Ph.D., and my mom was a career counselor with a master's in education and counseling psychology. They had the art and the science of life covered.

My dad is one of the smartest people I know. He's fiercely independent and always challenges "the system" because he is smart enough to do so and can back it up with his logic and reasoning. He is also never afraid to call out someone or something if he feels it is wrong, regardless of the professional consequences he might face. I got my drive and independence from him.

My mom, on the other hand, is acutely in tune with people's emotions and can assess situations and make adjustments to come to an agreement that works for everyone. From her, I got my empathy and opportunistic lens, which have served me so well over the years.

You never really know or appreciate what your parents do for you and the sacrifices they make when you're growing up. My goal now is to do my best to ensure that I have the same positive impact on my daughter that my parents had on me. Thanks, Mom and Dad. I love you.

Trish Bertuzzi

Trish Bertuzzi is the bestselling author of The Sales Development Playbook *and founder of the Bridge Group Inc. She and her team have worked with more than 380 business-to-business technology companies to help them unleash the power of inside sales. They are on a mission to help companies build repeatable pipelines and accelerate growth using both traditional and account-based strategies.*

....

I started my business in March 1998. I had a vision and a passion for helping business-to-business technology leaders build world-class inside sales teams. I had no fear of failure because I figured the worst thing that could happen would be that I would have to shut my doors and get another job.

Doors to The Bridge Group opened, and we did $300,000 in revenue in the first year. Does not sound like much. Apparently that is the magic number for an entrepreneur who is both selling and delivering services. I rolled into my second year with a full pipeline and a great attitude. I was cruising along until the third quarter, when all of a sudden I looked at my pipeline and it was non-existent. I had been so focused on delivery that I had taken my eye off the prospecting ball. Yikes!

I went into full-blown panic mode. I had no idea what to do. My existing contracts were coming to an end, and I had no firm projects in my line of sight. Holy crap—I was going to have to go get a job and give up my dream of being a successful female entrepreneur.

I literally could not get out of my own way to figure this out so I did what all smart women do. They call other smart women and ask for help. I called my friend Kristin Lembo, who is the CEO of Beyond Real Estate, and asked her to meet me for lunch. Now there is not much similarity between an inside sales consulting business and a real estate business. But Kristin is savvy, and I needed someone to listen to me and then give me a shove in the right direction.

And shove me she did. Kristin listened to my tale of woe. As I wound down, she looked across the table at me and said, "You know what to do, so do what you know." BAM! I heard her words and had an epiphany. I know what to do. I need to do what I tell my clients to do. Get on the damn phone and talk to people who might have a need for your service. In hindsight, it seems so silly. I was building a business teaching people how to use the phone to sell, but I was not doing it myself.

I went back to the office and built out a sales strategy that had me laser-focused on my target market. I crafted compelling messaging. I created an execution strategy that had me reaching out to CROs and CMOs on a regular basis. And you know what? It worked. Fast-forward to 2018, and I have a fifteen-person multimillion-dollar consulting practice.

Lesson learned? No matter how successful you are, spend part of every day working on pipeline. There is a phrase I love: Pipeline cures all ills. I am here to tell you that is the truth. Thanks, Kristin!

Randy Brandoff

Randy Brandoff is an accomplished innovator and builder of disruptive businesses. He founded Eleven James, a pioneering platform at the forefront of the luxury consumer evolution, after his tenure as chief marketing officer of NetJets, a Berkshire Hathaway company, where he served since 2010. He also helped launch Tequila Avion. Brandoff is on the Advisory Council for Entrepreneurship@Cornell and the entrepreneur board of Venture for America, a member of YPO, and an active angel investor to numerous early-stage ventures.

....

It's been my experience that true success in your career and life comes from following your passions, making your own decisions, and striving to constantly grow and evolve. If you're lucky, you'll find great mentors who actively guide and support you. Unless or until you find the right mentor, you can learn from almost everyone—even, and perhaps especially, when they don't know they're teaching.

Throughout my life, I have been fortunate to have been surrounded by extraordinary family members, friends, entrepreneurs, and executives—and astute enough to watch, study, strive to follow their most insightful spoken wisdom, and emulate their most remarkable characteristics.

Of all these exceptional people, the one who stands out as having the greatest impact on my life and career is the one who has been there literally since the beginning: my older brother Jared.

Since my earliest memories, Jared was my playmate and protector, and he set a remarkable example. A little over two years older than me, he was preternaturally mature and nurturing. I didn't realize it early on, but I was constantly learning and benchmarking.

I followed Jared to Cornell University and selected the same business major. While studying business, Jared was also pre-med, a computer science minor, and the president of our fraternity. He handled all those responsibilities as well as almost anyone could, but in the end, his lack of focus led to it taking a few extra years before he was accepted to medical school. The first lesson was that you can't do everything, at least not all at once. In life, you have to prioritize and make hard choices.

The second lesson was one of determination, persistence, and following your passion. Although Jared could have succeeded at anything he wanted to, he realized his heart was set on becoming a doctor, and he overcame every obstacle necessary until he achieved what he wanted. For entrepreneurs, successful prioritization is essential to survival. In addition, it takes great resolve to push beyond the unavoidable obstacles and temporary setbacks. If your heart isn't in it, it will never work.

Jared excelled in medicine and became an orthopedic spine surgeon. In the course of his medical studies, he married a terrific woman, and they had two wonderful boys. Jared was recruited by hospitals and medical practices from around the country but spurned significantly more lucrative opportunities elsewhere to remain in New York near his friends and family. When I asked him why he chose to stay, he memorably told me, "There's enough, and there's more than enough. I'm going to make enough staying here, and happiness is about a lot more than money."

Jared's decision demonstrated remarkable awareness, especially so early in his career and while he had a young family. He was right, of course, and during my years in private aviation, I came to know plenty of people who had achieved great wealth but were disillusioned when their wealth proved largely unfulfilling.

In my late twenties, I was blessed to meet a striking and formidable woman, Dayna, who I immediately knew was special and I hoped would be the one. Before long, our wedding day was approaching, and I was getting anxious because I couldn't get my head around the "till death do us part" commitment. Jared sensed my apprehension and said, "Don't think of this as a decision for the rest of your life. That thought process is inconsistent with how people live and behave. Ask yourself if there's any doubt in your mind about your decision and commitment today? Will there be any doubt tomorrow? This is a commitment you must make and reaffirm to yourself every day."

Eleven-plus years into a very strong marriage, I continue to confidently reaffirm my commitment every day. But I've also found tremendous application for this advice in entrepreneurship. Most people don't act on new business ideas because of how difficult it can be to make the leap and for fear of an unknown future. For those with truly groundbreaking concepts, it can be even harder because you're likely well ahead of everyone else in understanding the potential for your idea. I personally experienced this when launching Eleven James, and I used Jared's approach to carry on with confidence.

Prioritize, be passionate, endure, and check in on and reaffirm your commitment. All great lessons, but invariably there will be times where you just want to unplug and stop all the striving. That's OK and necessary. Just remember: There's likely someone who's watching and learning from you.

Marq Brown

Marq Brown is a lifelong athlete who played collegiate and professional football—for the Auburn Tigers and the New York Jets. After finishing his football career, he began a new career in the field of health and fitness, first as a personal trainer/manager of a facility and now as a "fitness curator." He spends most of his free time with his family. His accomplishments include All-SEC athlete in 2002, being named one of the top fitness experts in the Atlanta metro area, competing in endurance races, and being featured on the cover of the book Living With a SEAL, *written by his good friend Jesse Itzler.*

....

Dear football,

You've taught me so many things that at times it is hard to put into words what you have meant to me. Since May 19, 1980, my first day on this Earth, it's almost like our paths were destined to cross. I remember the first time I laid eyes on you; it was love at first sight. There was something about you that I was so drawn to. It was like I was made for you. Just a kid from the inner city of Paterson, New Jersey, I was born to a single, teenage mother, but in you I found my first friend and playmate. Those backyard reenactments of what I had watched on television every fall Sunday afternoon gave me the ability to escape and be whoever I idolized.

"Brown is at the 30, the 20, the 10—TOUCHDOWN!"

Even though I'd had a football in my hand since I could walk, we didn't officially meet until I was eight and my mom signed me up for Pop Warner football. I knew my father, but he was not always there, so you were the one constant I could count on. Just as you do for so many other kids, you took on a father role in my life and introduced me to a lot of strong men who would shape and mold me.

At an early age, you taught me the value of discipline, having a good work ethic, and teamwork, to name a few characteristics that I still value to this day. I took to you like a fish takes to water. I remember after a little league practice saying to my mom, "I'm going to play in the NFL one day." She said, "Only one in a million kids makes it," and I confidently replied, "I'm going to be that one!"

The older I got, the more I dedicated myself to our relationship. In high school while my friends were playing video games, I was putting in extra time to improve my skills on the football field in order to impress you. When my hard work began to pay off, it made me work even harder. As it often happens with a person's first love, you broke my heart! I remember it just like it was yesterday. It was the third game of my senior season, and I lay on the field in excruciating pain with a broken leg and heard the doctor say, "Your senior season is over." That experience, while devastating, taught me grit and how to fight back from adversity.

Football, you changed my life and opened so many doors for me. You showed me places I would not have ventured to go if not for you. You enabled me to gain a higher education as we continued our journey together at Auburn University, where I would meet my future wife and mother of my children. Lifelong friendships and bonds were made as I battled with and against other men who shared a similar relationship with you.

Unfortunately, more disappointment came after waiting two long days to hear my name called during the NFL draft, but that never happened. There were two options: feel sorry for myself or figure out another way to reach my goal. Falling back on lessons of perseverance you had taught me, I eventually made my lifelong dream a reality when I became a member of the New York Jets as an undrafted free agent in 2002. How ironic is it that our home games were played at Meadowlands Stadium, less than twenty miles from where I was born? Talk about coming full circle. You were my destiny.

To this day, I still apply what I learned from you in business and in life. I can't wait to share our experiences, the good and the bad, with my children. Even though my playing days are long gone, you will always hold a special place in my heart.

There is one thing for certain: My life would not have turned out the same if we had never met, and for that I will always be grateful.

Love always,

Just a kid from Paterson, New Jersey

Dana Cavalea

Dana Cavalea spent twelve years with the New York Yankees, mostly as director of strength and conditioning and performance enhancement. He received MLB's 2009 Nolan Ryan Award, given to the top strength coach by his peers. Cavalea has trained greats such as Alex Rodriguez, Derek Jeter, Mariano Rivera, Andy Pettitte, and Justin Verlander, and is now a speaker and consultant to professional athletes, executives, and universities on stress reduction, and improving work/life balance, and daily performance/outcomes.

....

As we go through life, we go through phases. Through many of those early phases of life, we think we know everything. We actually believe we can get through the battle alone.

But we soon come to realize, through all of life's trials and tribulations, that is certainly not the case. At least not for me.

My early dreams were filled with visions of playing baseball for the New York Yankees. I wasn't sure at the time whether I would make it as a first baseman, an outfielder, or possibly even a catcher. Big decisions to make for a kid swinging a waffle-ball bat on the front lawn of his parents' house.

Replaying and rehearsing myself making that game-winning hit in the bottom of the ninth, clearing the bases and culminating in a Yankees win. That was my life. Dreaming that the impossible was possible.

There is nothing you can't do. But if you want it, you are going to have to work for it. And by work, I am not talking about strictly the labor, but visionary work.

This is where my mom comes in.

When I was asked to write a piece about the most influential person in my life in terms of life successes and who I am today, I had to go with Mom.

A mother, teacher, and most important my personal motivator, she never lets me get lazy. She never lets me fall behind. And one thing is for sure, she never lets me make an excuse of being too busy, too tired, or too anything.

As a young guy who grew up shy, I was told one thing over and over: "Dana, if you are going to make it in this world, you better have moxie, kid."

My mother grew up in Queens, New York — home of the American hustler. If you want something, you better go get it. There are no handouts in this world, and nobody is sitting around all day thinking about you getting to the next level.

So I went. I took my act to South Florida, where I got an education, confidence, and my dream.

As I mentioned earlier, I knew I was going to make it to the Yankees. When I was a kid, all you had to do was ask me. I just didn't realize it wouldn't be as a first baseman, an outfielder, or a catcher. I found the fastest way without the long minor league bus rides — as a strength and conditioning coach.

I got the gig when I was nineteen years old and went from intern to head coach in four short years. How, you ask?

Simple. I listened to my mom.

"What is the worst thing anybody could ever tell you, Dana? No. So you better go put yourself out there and ask."

That's my mom. All guts, all glory. The ability to speak to anybody in a fearless manner.

Facing rejection? Ha.

"What is rejection?" she would ask.

I took that advice, and Brian Cashman, the GM of the Yankees, gave me a shot.

Best gamble either of us ever took.

So in life, you must always remember that to achieve anything great, you will have to put yourself out there. You must get comfortable hearing the word "no." But for every NO there may just be a YES that will change your life. That's what happened to me. It can happen to you.

Thanks Mom.

Todd Cohen

Todd Cohen is the nation's leading voice on building a sales culture. He is the principal of Sales Leader LLC and author of Everyone's in Sales *and* Stop Apologizing and Start Selling. *He is a regular contributor to* The Huffington Post *and* Philadelphia Business Journal, *as well as dozens of trade and association magazines, and publishes the monthly* Sales Culture Newsletter.

....

When I was asked to write this essay on who I wanted to give a standing O, there were many amazing people who came to mind and from whom I could choose. I wish I could write something meaningful for everyone who has meant so much to me. So many people have been significant in my life.

I started thinking about what I have learned that has helped me along the way. After some soul searching, the answer came relatively quickly. The best gifts I have learned are those of humility, vulnerability, and presence. They are cousins of one another, and the combination of these human traits—gifts, if you will—is a valuable and priceless currency.

That brings me to where I started to learn and observe how those human behaviors work. Again, the answer was easy. My father, Marvin Cohen, taught me to be approachable, real, and decent. I speak of him often in my keynotes and workshops, and my first book, *Everyone's in Sales,* has many stories of how I learned to be who I am.

Born and raised in Pittsburgh, my father had a rough childhood. When he was an infant, his father died, and his mother placed him in an orphanage when he was a child because she couldn't afford to keep him. After high school, my father went into the Air Force, where he learned photography. In later years, he built a modest business as a wedding photographer.

As a child, I spent countless hours listening to him sell his services to prospective brides and grooms. He was successful because he was genuine and humble. It was so much more than his technical skills. My father was always approachable, and when talking with people, he focused his attention on them. He was present with people, and that inspired them to trust him with the most important day of their lives.

My father had an easy laugh and could make other people laugh. His way with people was one of vulnerability and realness that drew them in. They wanted to talk with him, and the relationships he had were stronger and better because he could be vulnerable.

Vulnerability is a rare skill, and it was part of his DNA. Vulnerable people are not afraid to show their emotions. He never failed to show me how he felt about me, and he could express feelings. Too often people are busy trying to be something they are not. Dad was not afraid to show who he was. He was flawed and not without problems. He was perfectly imperfect. He was also acutely aware of his flaws. His ability to talk about himself and who he was made me unafraid to be the same way. He was also not afraid to be himself. That vulnerability translated into a presence that endeared him in a genuine way to people. His clients liked that he was always with them and only them.

I often say that if you want to sell yourself, you need to engage more. Engagement means being someone people are comfortable walking up to. It also says you have to be someone who is self-aware of when you are and are not approachable. I have so many memories of asking my dad tough questions about our family, his problems, and other topics that kids usually don't think to ask. He always stopped what he was doing, physically turned to look at me, listened intently, and answered honestly.

Marvin Cohen's natural ease with being vulnerable made him approachable. That approachability was possible because he was present with those around him. He won healthy relationships, respect, and trust. He also earned a son's love and respect.

Joe De Sena

Joe De Sena is the founder and CEO of Spartan, the world's largest obstacle race and endurance brand. After building a multimillion-dollar business in college and creating a Wall Street trading firm, De Sena moved his family to Vermont, to operate an organic farm, a bed and breakfast, and a general store for hikers, while building a passion for ultramarathons, adventure races, and endurance events, leading to the idea for Spartan. De Sena is the New York Times *bestselling author of* Spartan Up *and* Spartan Fit*, and his third book,* The Spartan Way*, is scheduled for release in September 2018.*

....

Do I have to pick just one person? Yikes. I've had so many influences throughout my life, and all have propelled me forward in a slightly different way.

Here at Spartan, I meet some of the most inspiring people in the world every day, and each one teaches me a little something about being a better leader and person.

Of course, I wouldn't be writing this today if it weren't for the people who encouraged me at an early age to work hard, embrace adversity, and always be myself.

My father was a relentless workhorse who taught me to keep going until the job is done—not when the clock says it's time to punch out.

My neighbor, the boss of an organized-crime family, taught me to always keep my word and exceed expectations. This lesson was paramount when I started my own pool-cleaning business and it still is today.

When I got to college, I was already doing pretty well for myself as a professional pool cleaner. So well, in fact, that I was ready to leave school and move on to something new. Luckily, my buddy Al insisted I finish school. He taught me persistence and grit when I was ready to quit.

But there's one person who taught me the most valuable lesson of all—my mom. Not only did she teach me to do the right thing even when other people weren't, but she pushed me to become the independent, freewheeling person I am today.

Jean De Sena was not your normal mother from Queens. She was into yoga, meditation, and vegan food in an all-Italian neighborhood. She ran ten miles a day back when folks used their Cadillacs to drive ten feet. She was always focused on health, wellness, and helping others—even when our neighbors thought she was just plain weird.

My sister and I were embarrassed by our mom's eccentricities, and we tried our hardest to blend in with the rest of the neighborhood kids. We were ashamed to bring friends over for fear that we'd open the front door to find a bunch of monks chanting in the living room. At lunch, we'd try to hide our branch-filled sandwiches as everyone else chowed down on meatball subs.

When I was thirteen, my mother and father divorced, and Mom moved us to Ithaca, New York, to start fresh. Of course, at the time, this was just another reminder that mom wasn't like the rest of our friends' parents.

Starting over in a new place was difficult. We didn't know anyone, and the community was very different from our rough Queens neighborhood. I was lonely and a little lost, and I started to depend heavily on my mom. One day, when I was in high school, I came home to find the deadbolt locked. I checked the back door, but it was locked, too. I tried to pry open the garage door, but it wouldn't budge. I checked every single window, but they were all closed and locked. I had no key and no way of getting in.

As I peered through the living room window, I saw my mom stretched out in downward dog on her yoga mat. I knocked, but her focus remained on her practice. She looked completely at peace as I desperately attempted to get her attention.

We went on like this for an entire week—her ignoring me as I banged on the doors and windows. I rolled up in a sweatshirt and slept in the backyard. I searched for scraps of food and ended up desperately munching on blades of grass to satiate my hunger. It wasn't until I was able to creep up and sneak in the door behind her on the seventh day that the two of us came face to face.

"We need to talk," Mom said.

"The free ride is over," she told me. "You're old enough to take responsibility for your actions and help out around this house."

It may sound crazy, but after being locked out of the house for an entire week, mom's words hit me like the proverbial ton of bricks. She was right. I had come to expect that my house, my family, and a twig sandwich would always be waiting for me at home, but I needed to stop taking things for granted. I couldn't rely on my mother to become the man I wanted to be—I needed to make it happen. I needed to stop worrying what everyone else thought and use my gut as my guardrails. I agreed to get a job and pay for my own groceries and paper products immediately.

When mom locked me out of the house, she wanted to teach me independence, but she taught me a lot more than just that. From that day on, I knew that I needed to be self-reliant—to make my own decisions and embrace my differences.

I still use this lesson today in my business and with my family. My kids probably have felt the same way my sister and I used to about our mom's quirkiness, but I wouldn't have it any other way. Everything we do—all day, every day—is outside the norm. Whether we're climbing mountains in our pajamas or hiking through freezing waterfalls with the marathon monks in Japan, my kids already know who they are, and they're not afraid of being a little different.

Karen Dillon

Karen Dillon is a former editor of Harvard Business Review *and co-author of the* New York Times *bestseller* How Will You Measure Your Life? *with Clayton Christensen, as well as the forthcoming* Prosperity Paradox *(HarperCollins, January 2019), also with Christensen.*

Meeting Clayton Christensen changed my life.

You might think that was because I had the good fortune to meet and spend hours talking with Clay, one of the world's most respected thought leaders, about his theory of disruptive innovation or the many people and companies he has helped along the way. But that's not why he changed my life.

In Spring 2010, as the editor of *Harvard Business Review* magazine, I had been casting around for an article that would add a little extra something to our Summer 2010 double issue. I realized that the students about to graduate from Harvard Business School that spring had applied to business school when the economy was still rosy and everything seemed possible—but they were now graduating into a world of uncertainty. I phoned one of the co-presidents of the graduating HBS class to pick his brain for ideas. It was he who first told me that Clay had been selected by the class to address them and that his words had been extraordinarily moving.

So I tracked Clay down and asked if I could come by his office to try to capture some of what he had told the students. He willingly obliged, and I traipsed across campus with a digital recorder and the sole agenda of getting an article for my magazine.

When I walked into his office, I was thinking only about the lives of graduating MBA students. When I emerged an hour or so later, I was thinking about my own.

Every question Clay asked and every theory he discussed resonated with me. As I've reviewed the transcript of our original conversation in the years since then, I can see the discussion peppered with my own evolving thoughts. Was I actually allocating my resources to the things that mattered most to me? Did I have a strategy for my life? Did I have a purpose? How would I measure my life?

I stood in the parking lot of HBS a few hours later and knew I didn't like my answers to those questions. Since then, I have changed almost everything about my life with the goal of refocusing on my family. I resigned from *Harvard Business Review* in the spring of 2011 with the good wishes of my colleagues and have spent the years since then pursuing a patchwork of writing and other opportunities to create, while simultaneously being truly present in the moments of my own life—and, more important, in the lives of my husband and daughters. I've written two bestselling books with Clay (and we're working on our third collaboration as I write this), I've had the good fortune to travel both with my family and for work to parts of the world I had only dreamed of knowing, and I have come to truly know and value my children as individuals. I haven't regretted a single decision I've made since the day I first left Clay's office.

I consider myself lucky to have had the invaluable benefit of a private tutorial in the theories of Clayton Christensen. But more important, I consider myself privileged to have had the chance to collaborate with a man who is brilliant, kind, and generous not some of the time, not much of the time, but *all* of the time. A man who made me see my own life through a new set of lenses—and that has made all the difference.

Dr. Howard Dover

Dr. Howard Dover is the director of the Center for Professional Sales, clinical professor of marketing, and sales coach at the University of Texas at Dallas. As the director he consults with the center's partners on how to identify and coach new sales professionals. His expertise includes digital disruption, sales enablement, social selling, and sales effectiveness strategies. He is the resident technology expert for Sales Educator's Academy and has been an invited speaker at numerous sales, sales educator, and marketing conferences.

. . . .

In life, there are what I like to call "pivotal moments" that shape who we are and who we will become.

My father ran away from home during the Great Depression and volunteered for the Army during World War II. Although my mother attended a community college, my father never finished high school. They provided a humble home where values were taught in our family. How does one come from such a home to become a business professor?

Leonard Ellis was my best friend's dad, a successful businessman, a great father, and a respected church leader. Mr. Ellis had a significant influence on my early years. He taught me key business concepts, to be mindful of my physical appearance, and to love my family. During my post-high school year, he pulled me aside one night and asked me what I was doing with my life. He then challenged me and committed me to accelerate my plans to serve a mission. He helped me recognize that my mindset was hindering me and that it was time to act. This moment was pivotal to me serving a mission.

Farrell Smith was the president of the Vienna, Austria, mission where I served as a missionary for the Church of Jesus Christ of Latter Day Saints. At the end of my mission, I had an exit interview with President Smith. In that interview, he asked me about my future plans. I had plans to go back to California and work but no plans for college. President Smith looked me in the eyes and said, "The brethren of our church ask me to share that they expect three things of you.... Third, seek and obtain a higher education."

Honestly, my heart sank! I had not planned nor was I really open to going to college. But I was also pliable and coachable when President Smith asked me to consider going to Brigham Young University. I am sure he could see that I had no interest in pursuing an education, but he stepped up and delivered a valuable message that was pivotal in my decision to seek a higher education.

Amy Marsh was a nursing student who worked full-time at a residential care facility for children with disabilities. During the week of Valentine's Day, I met Amy, who would truly change my life forever. At the time, I owned my own business and was attending school out of obligation and not overly focused on my studies. Amy was a 4.0 student in nursing who challenged me with words and association to become better and engage more in my academic and professional endeavors.

After some time dating, she agreed to marry me. I am fortunate to have met my intellectual companion early in my life. My wife is my best friend, a capable leader, a mother, and my partner in all aspects of life. Meeting Amy challenged me to become a lifelong learner and to always strive to be a worthy husband and father.

Dr. Mark Showalter was a tenure-track economics professor at Brigham Young University when I met him during my undergraduate studies. He was the kind of professor you rarely meet. Mark had a desire to see his students learn, which motivated me to be a better student and stretch my mind. After graduation, he was an invaluable source and resource about the journey to obtain a doctoral degree. When graduate school was challenging, Mark provided the needed encouragement to understand why the challenge was essential to achieving my objective. Mark's coaching and mentoring helped set an example for me on how to be a good academic mentor to others.

How does a young man from a non-degreed working-class home become a nationally recognized business professor? By having key people step up at the pivotal moments of his life and make a difference. Sometimes it is the little moments when we give of our time that will make a lasting impact on others. That is what has happened in my life, and I endeavor to pay it forward.

Stacy Feiner

Stacy Feiner is a business psychologist who helps business owners get the results they want faster by addressing the interplay of leadership, business, and psychology. Feiner has introduced business psychology to Fortune 100 corporations, academic institutions, and closely-held companies. She is a national speaker, blogger, and author of Talent Mindset: The Business Owner's Guide to Building Bench Strength.

....

"Just because a million people think something is a good idea doesn't make it a good idea." I was eight years old when my father clipped that quote from the newspaper for me. He knew these words would speak to me. Little did I know that they would define my life and career.

When I was growing up, my parents made us aware of social injustices. Dinnertime was when we discussed our responsibility to right them. Words mattered, and we dug into them. These experiences empowered me. I gravitated to serious issues and relished conversations where solutions emerged. I was able to see things others couldn't and bring them into view.

Early on, the problem I often ran into was that my insights challenged the status quo. They made people feel uncomfortable and sometimes exposed. When I got to college, Dr. Lee Quinby, an intensely motivating and demanding professor, pointed out that I had a gift for being provocative with observations and penetrating with insights, and that in time, I would make this my calling. That's when my trajectory became clear. I became a psychologist and learned to harness this gift with a sophistication and pace that can draw people in, help them find the right words, and compel them to be engaged.

Many times over the years, I learned that standing up for my ideals could incite backlash from others. Yet looking back, I also see that it deepened every meaningful relationship I've had. I was drawn to concepts about human potential, winning against the odds, and personal growth. Initially, I was drawn to the complex and intimate work with family systems as a psychotherapist. Eventually, I found that my real passion was to bring psychology to business systems, where I would have a bigger impact on improving the human condition.

By now I've listened to hundreds of business owners talk about deeply personal experiences owning and running their own companies. They are providers to families, leaders of companies, and stewards of a legacy. An entire ecosystem of people depends on their effectiveness. And since 65 percent of our U.S. population is employed by privately owned firms—giving them a unique opportunity to improve the health of our nation—I engineered a coaching method specific to their needs. By blending psychology, business, and leadership, my method accelerates a business owner's ability to achieve goals. The stakes are high. Coaching is the conduit for leaders to live their power.

Growth is achieved by digging deep. And you don't do it alone.

- First, realize you can and must be great. But don't expect to be inspired. Realizations come from being challenged.
- Grapple with new ideas, untangle from old assumptions, use better words, and try new moves. Remember that how you define a problem determines how you solve it.
- Commit every day to doing better than yesterday. Don't wait. Expect others to do the same.
- Use your power and privilege to build strong teams and create environments where people do their best work. Nurturing the community you lead is a bottom-line requirement.
- Think big. Profitable companies with engaged employees improve the health of our nation.
- Be a force with a mission and a cause. Embody your greatness.

My work gives me the great privilege to pay it forward, ensuring that the worthy ideals and missions of others are not abandoned but realized.

Nothing could be better than tapping into our deepest strengths and calling out those strengths in fellow humans.

Just because a million people think something is a good idea doesn't make it a good idea. A loud and resounding standing O to Dr. Lee Quinby and all those who taught me that to win in life, you must have the confidence to deliver on your own ideals.

Jen Fitzpatrick

Jen Fitzpatrick (aka Jenny Fitz) is a mother of two incredible boys, TEDx speaker, international bestselling author, educator, co-founder of the Hero Intelligence Agency, business coach, marketing director, professional photographer, certified wedding planner, humanitarian, and advocate for the rights of women and children. When she isn't seeking and sharing stories of real-life superheroes, organizing charity events, or volunteering, she can be found enjoying networking and helping other entrepreneurs discover their why.

....

When I reflect on all the life lessons I have learned and the people who have shared their wisdom and inspiration with me, it becomes apparent that I have had the most incredible people guiding me along my path of discovery and purpose. One particular woman I owe a great deal of this discovery to is Sheryl Taylor.

Sheryl and I met just over fifteen years ago in a small community in the Eastern Townships in Quebec. I had landed my first full-time teaching position at Butler Elementary, and Sheryl was the resource teacher. When I first met her, Sheryl's fashion sense, her contagious laughter, and her selflessness projected an indescribable radiance that you only come to know when you meet her face to face.

After telling her my life experiences up until that point, she took me under her wing and so the friendship began. A few months later, I found myself residing on Sheryl's futon in her living room after the relationship I was in had ended and I had nowhere to live for the remainder of the school year. During that emotional time, Sheryl encouraged me to figure out what I really wanted out of life, and she also introduced me to mindfulness, awareness, and true compassion.

Fast-forward a year and I found myself living and teaching in London,

England. Sheryl made the trip across the big pond to visit, and we continued our hilarious and multi-venturous journey around the countryside. Sheryl taught me to laugh at even the most mundane situations and find gratitude in the little things. I didn't realize until years later that the conversations we had during that trip would contribute to my pursuit of entrepreneurship.

After I left the teaching profession in 2009 and pursued my own company, Sheryl was there to advise, encourage, and provide a listening ear during the highs and the lows of just starting out. She taught me to fail gracefully and never give up on my dreams. We both share the same ideology that if you are kind, compassionate, and generous, you will come to realize what is most important in life.

Even though there is a thirty-year age difference between us, I don't just consider Sheryl my mentor and life coach, but I consider her a dear friend. We have shared similar experiences in life and business, and because of Sheryl, I have been able to create a path of discovering my own "why" and the type of legacy I want to leave. I would not be where I am today if Sheryl had not taken me under her wing all those years ago.

If I were to reflect on all the things that Sheryl has taught me, I would have to say that the one that stands out is not to be afraid of trying something new. If you have a passion, an interest, or an idea that is bubbling inside you, then you can only really know what your true potential is by taking a chance and following your dreams. I am forever grateful for the opportunities that I have had because of this life lesson.

Over the last decade, Sheryl has been an advocate, friend, confidante, and incredible support. She listens to my ridiculous ideas and gives her opinion in such a way that I know becoming an entrepreneur was always the path I was supposed to take. The best part is that Sheryl recently started on her own entrepreneurial path after retiring from education, and so the adventure continues!

Candice Galek

Candice Galek is the founder and CEO of Bikini Luxe, a designer women's swimwear retailer. After becoming the most viewed person on LinkedIn due to her unique marketing techniques, she built her personal brand and shared her experiences via her column at Inc.com, featuring guests such as Dr. Deepak Chopra, Seth Godin, and Simon Sinek. Galek was a featured honoree on the Forbes 30 Under 30 list and has expanded into public speaking and business coaching.

....

It's true what they say: Hindsight is 20/20. I invited my mom to brunch recently, and she asked me what my take on my childhood was. It was something that I had put a lot of thought into, and I could proudly say that I was grateful for how I was raised.

I learned important skills that to this day I cherish and feel gave me an advantage over my competition in the business world. I had a fun childhood where my creativity ran wild. It was full of climbing trees, catching lizards, turning cardboard boxes into doll houses, and bringing home stray animals. I thought I had the best life a kid could possibly have.

She looked at me with teary eyes and said, "You know, I've always wondered what you thought of your childhood and if you ever felt as though you'd missed out on anything." For some reason, we were both in tears at the table of a restaurant in South Beach, but it felt good.

We then discussed my teenage years, and she seems to remember them through rose-colored glasses, which I am thankful for because, quite honestly, I was a bit of a handful. I played multiple varsity sports, and by the age of sixteen, I had two jobs on top of that so I kept quite busy, and boy, was I tired (and hungry) by the time I finally got home.

I understood the importance of having a job—and actually wanted to work—because a strong work ethic had been ingrained in me. As we were having our heart-to-heart, she told me that she was glad that I had a happy upbringing because in reality some days she had to decide how to put food on the table. She knew the bills came first, and once those were taken care of, she thought to herself, "OK, I have $30 to feed this voracious little blonde-haired girl for a couple of weeks. How do I do this?"

I didn't know we were poor, but in these moments, she taught me one of my favorite lessons: how to stretch a dollar. My beautiful mother raised me on her own. At one point, she worked at IHOP, which I thought was great because I got to eat all the chocolate chips I could handle. But her dream was to be a police officer. She knew that wouldn't be feasible because I still needed so much of her attention, so she put it off until I was older.

When the time came that I was able to get myself to and from school, she pulled me aside and told me about her dream to be a police officer and asked my permission to make that happen. I told her, "Of course!" and she hugged me tight. In that moment, I realized the sacrifice she had made in order to raise me to the best of her ability.

I look back on these years being raised by a single mother as some of the best in my life. I thought she was the coolest person in the world. I watched her like a hawk, and she unknowingly taught me many lessons along the way that would stick with me well into adulthood, such as:

1. How to give a strong handshake.
2. How to be self-sufficient—and when to ask for help.
3. To have respect for myself and know that it is vital to do so before I can respect others.
4. Not to lie, cheat, or steal because it always comes back to bite you in the butt.
5. How to communicate my feelings and talk things through to find a resolution.
6. I don't have to be friends with everyone, but I do have to be nice to them.
7. Money doesn't grow on trees; if I want something, I have to work for it.
8. Anything boys can do, girls can do better.

9. Being frugal is a lifestyle choice, and saving money never goes out of style.
10. I am in control of my life and can make it whatever I want it to be.

Did you know that, statistically, children raised in single-parent households are more likely to become drug-dependent, commit suicide, continue a cycle of poverty, experience violence, commit a crime, or underperform in school? The lessons I learned from my loving mother helped shape the person I am today, and together we overcame the odds and have both made our dreams a reality with each other's support.

Noah Goldman

Noah Goldman helps software-as-a-service companies with sales process, lead generation, and team formation. He has worked in both business-to-business and business-to-consumer tech companies, from marketing to finance and corporate development. He is the host of the Enterprise Sales *podcast, which features the smartest people in sales. He honed his podcast skills during a prior life in TV production. He holds an MBA from Vanderbilt University and a bachelor's degree from Syracuse University.*

....

A standing O for my "family": love, even when it hurts.

I'll be the first so say I'm not easy to love.

As the only child of a single mom, I was wild.

All the time.

I still remember the time my mom lost sight of me in a mall and chastised me for getting lost. She was so angry and at the same time so worried.

I didn't understand what the big deal was at the time.

As I grew up, things seemed tumultuous, perhaps more so than they were in a more objective reality not held by the perception of a six-year-old.

I would get in fights with my mom, not really realizing why we were doing it. At the time, it seemed important.

Eventually, I grew to get pretty angry about it all—piss and vinegar.

My mom—bless her friggin' heart—still loved me.

There were times I probably made myself so angry I couldn't stand it.

She still loved me.

Maybe that's the job moms do, I suppose.

But I dunno.

I definitely didn't deserve it.

A friend of mine said it best, though: Family is who will love you even when they don't like you.

Let that one sink in for a moment.

By this definition, your "family" can be anyone.

That friend who let you crash on his couch when you had nowhere else to go—thanks, Steve—that's "family."

Your "rotten," "no good," "good-for-nothing" cousins? Those are just "relatives."

But you can love them, too, and probably should.

At low points in my life, I definitely withdrew and lashed out.

My once silver tongue turned to acid.

I just didn't care.

It really is amazing I had anyone left around me at some points.

Again, I definitely did not deserve it.

Yes, family is who will love you even when they don't like you.

Friends—they will just love you as long as they happen to like you.

Several years back, I lost my job.

I was a mess.

I stumbled into a puddle of depression and despondency.

Not pretty.

One by one, my so-called friends, my network abandoned me—or so it seemed.

"How can I help?" I would ask and inevitably would never hear back.

As the angst got worse, you could say I was not the most endearing person.

Certain relatives wouldn't return my calls.

Again, I don't blame them, but it showed me where they stood.

But my "family" was always—ALWAYS—there.

Matt let me work out for free at his gym for awhile. Brooke bought me lunch.

They survived me when I wasn't worth surviving and barely could myself.

More than that, they are the reason I am here today.

That scholarly chanteur Marilyn Manson, of all people, said it right: "If you want to find out who your real friends are, sink the ship. The first ones to jump aren't your friends."

He's right, of course, but more than that, they aren't your "family."

So I want to give a standing O to my "family."

They taught me what it means to love.

You have to love even when it really, really, REALLY hurts.

They say when you need a friend, you can never find one. But when you seek to BE a friend, they are everywhere.

And that's true.

But I think that's a low bar.

Where possible, don't just seek to be a friend.

Seek to be "family."

The cost is high. The work is terrible. The pay is even worse.

But the rewards are phenomenal.

Marc Hodulich

Marc Hodulich is general manager and operating partner at Be Boundless, where he manages the business interests for serial entrepreneur Jesse Itzler, co-owner of the Atlanta Hawks. Previously, Hodulich founded multiple nationwide event series, including BeerFit and the Wall Street Decathlon, which raised millions of dollars for charity while garnering coverage from Sports Illustrated, The Wall Street Journal, *and ESPN. He is based in Atlanta, Georgia, where he lives with his wife, sons, and dog Barkley.*

....

In high school, I was a runner. I guess I still am, but back in 1996, it defined me. As one friend put it: "Michael Jordan dunks. 2Pac raps. You run."

I was starting to find my way in high school and running was separating me from my peers. It gave me purpose and a sense of pride. And most of all, I truly loved it.

It seems every aspiring runner at some point goes through the Steve Prefontaine phase. Prefontaine was a legend and still is. He made running cool. He was Nike's first athlete. Think about that for a second: *Nike's* first athlete. Steve was daring and ran a race not to see who was the fastest but who had the most guts. It was about being daring and willing to take risks and push through the pain that separated Steve from all others. I translated this as: Be willing to hurt more than the others and you'll win. The problem was that I didn't know the difference between pain and injury.

It was May 1996 and track season was in full swing. I was winning races and challenging seniors for state titles. I was driven to win and test myself. I had a plan: Build off a great sophomore season, win some state titles, and run at an elite Division 1 school. But as Mike Tyson once said, "Everyone has a plan until they get punched in the mouth."

My sucker punch came in the form of a subtle yet growing pain in the top of my foot. Fight through the pain, I told myself. When the pain escalated, I'd stick my foot in a bucket of water to ease the swelling and numb the pain. When my mom caught wind of this, she made me see a sports medicine specialist. Some quick X-rays showed a stress fracture, while a CT scan showed something much worse. I had not only been running on a broken foot for months, but the bone was dead and could not heal on its own. Worse yet, it was the tarsal navicular, the same injury that had ended Bill Walton's and Yao Ming's careers.

The first doctor I saw was highly experienced, respected, and wise beyond his years. The prognosis was simple: He could fix my broken foot, but I'd never run competitively again. My stride, foot strike, and constant pounding were too much for a brittle bone to handle. To say a few tears were shed is like saying the Cubs winning the World Series was a nice win for the franchise.

There was no hope. My dreams were shattered, and my ignorance of running through the pain was the culprit. It didn't seem fair. I can't imagine how hard this was for my parents. Seeing their joy and excitement when I ran fueled me. It was something we shared as a family. And now it was gone. Or was it?

My parents agreed that a second opinion was needed and sought out an up-and-coming sports medicine group run by Dr. James Andrews. Anyone who was anyone in sports got their work done there. Bo Jackson, Roger Clemens, Troy Aikman. My parents and I met with a young orthopedic surgeon, Dr. Jeff Davis. I will never forget our consultations with him. He was direct. He was honest. He was confident. He was unconventional. And he was optimistic.

Dr. Davis gave me the one thing that anyone feeling down, hurt, sick, lonely, desperate, or distraught needs: hope. He had a plan. It wasn't without risk, but with risk comes reward. The downside could not be worse than not running again. And the upside? Boundless.

The plan was to shave bone from my shin and insert it in the void in my foot to spur new growth. Then take screws to rejoin the bones and employ a rigorous rehab protocol. It should have all been daunting, but his confidence and willingness to try something new erased all doubts.

Dr. Davis' approach to my problem had a profound impact on me. My business partner, Jesse Itzler, says, "Normal is broken," and he's right. I learned that at fifteen and just didn't realize it. Dr. Davis didn't follow the normal procedure. He was willing to fight convention. He was willing to take a risk, with me, for a worthy outcome. And it paid off.

Post-surgery I was able to win five state titles and run for Auburn University's track and field team. I have completed an Ironman Triathlon and pushed a quadriplegic in a wheelchair in the Marine Corps Marathon. But more than that, I have never settled. I have a wonderful wife, Stacey, and two amazing boys, Chase and Dylan. I have an amazing business partner and businesses I am proud of. A second opinion changed my life. And for that I thank my parents.

Dr. Davis deserves a standing O but not for his groundbreaking surgery or my recovery. That misses the point. My life trajectory changed based on the way he approached and solved my problem with confidence, humility, and courage. Thank you, Dr. Davis. I am forever grateful.

Philippe Hoerle-Guggenheim

Philippe Hoerle-Guggenheim was raised in Bonn, Germany, where he was exposed to the creative arts through his mother and maternal grandmother, a noted antique and art collector. After graduating from Anglia Ruskin University, Cambridge he worked at Ernst and Young and the Hyatt Corporation but stayed tethered to the art world by hosting events for artists in the U.S. and Europe. Hoerle-Guggenheim's reputation for bold, provocative, distinct artists was established with HG Contemporary's inaugural group exhibition in 2014 featuring artist RETNA.

....

Life takes turns—straight turns, wide turns, symbolic turns, love turns, hungry turns, lost turns, winning turns, ugly turns, beautiful turns. We define turns, and we are defined by turns. Every turn has a greater significance in life than at first perceivable. What appears to be a negative turn can very well be a positive one. You have no control over the turns that come at you, but you have control over what to do with a turn and how to turn bad into good, good into bad. Every turn has its meaning.

There is no mastery class to life. You live, you exist, you persist, and one day, you will look back at all the turns you have taken and see what connected them all. In hindsight, you want to know that it all made sense. On every turn, you were shaped, made, and molded into who you have become. There are blessings in every turn no matter how you look at it. You win or you learn, but you never lose.

Look up the meaning of the word "turn": "an act of moving something in a circular direction around an axis or point." An axis or point—not a beginning or an end. An axis or point that stays the same, and you turn and move around it yet you always stay connected. As life goes in turns, it changes, lessons are learned, and growth is experienced. You turn in various directions and change constantly, but the axis and point stay the same.

My standing O goes to my axis, my platform, my stability. My inner self that insisted on a better life. The silent hours when yet another turn went from bad to worse, yet you patiently waited for the greatness that brews inside you. The axis that exists inside me that wants more and expects more of myself. The rock-solid foundation that is unbreakable, unshakeable, and protected through my relationship with God. You can't control the turns, but you can control the power, firmness, and dedication of the axis you stay connected to.

It seems as though this would be a standing O to myself, a form of conceited self-importance. But nothing could be further from the truth. Nothing shaped me more than the turns my life took and continues to take. The many who impacted a turn, for good or bad, were there for a reason. They shaped my WHY. Now approached with expectancy and joy, I know the power of my axis.

It wasn't a sole person for me but the multitude of turns in my life that made me the best version of myself that I am today and the better version I will be tomorrow. Further, while I feel blessed and grateful for the realization of my WHY and my axis, I feel it's a celebration of something that was placed within me by someone else, something bigger. Isn't the second most important day in your life, after you were born, the day you realized why? Turns get you there. They are an expression of the connection we all have.

When your next turn comes into place, stay firm, stay fearless, and protect your axis, not your turns. Protect your foundation, and the best is yet to come.

Merril Hoge

Former NFL running back Merril Hoge was an analyst at ESPN for twenty-one years and helped launch ESPN 2, NFL Live, and Fantasy Football, along with being part of the longest-running NFL show on television, NFL Matchup. Hoge is chairman of the board of the Highmark Caring Foundation, which has created four centers in Pennsylvania for grieving children, adolescents, and their families who have lost loved ones. He published his first book, Find a Way: Three Words That Changed My Life, *in 2010. It is about the philosophy that has guided him and enabled him to overcome obstacles throughout his life.*

....

Find A Way. Those words have helped me live a dream and fight to live. When I was twelve, I had a wall of cork in my bedroom where I would pin my goals. One day I was looking at my main goal: "I will play in the NFL." And I started to think of all the things people would say to me after I answered their question: "What do you want to do when you grow up?" When I told them I was going to play in the NFL, they would counter with: 1) Oh, son, do you know how hard that is? 2) Do you know what the odds are of you playing in the NFL? 3) Don't put all your eggs in one basket; I would not want you to be disappointed. 4) That's impossible!

The more I thought about what people said to me, the more my goal was nothing more than words on a wall. Then my first moment of truth in life came. As I let my mind fill with the negative things everyone had been saying to me, the words "Find A Way" popped into my head. My thought process instantly changed. Those words inspired me to take action. I will never forget the change I felt not just in my thoughts, but the energy in my body. I was so moved by those words that I got down from my bed and wrote the words "Find a Way" in blue on an extra 10x12 card and put that at the top of the corked wall with all my goals below it. Those words inspired a journey.

I'm a product of a lot of people who inspired me directly or indirectly and who challenged me. The one person who had a significant impact at this first moment of truth in my life was Walter Payton. Those words inspired me to ask who was doing what I wanted to do and how could they help me? My first thought was Payton. I had watched every game of his that I could, and I had read everything I could find about him, but there had to be more. I remember this being said about Payton: He was not the biggest, the strongest, or even the fastest—he was just the best.

At the time, I thought everyone who was the best had to be the biggest, strongest, and fastest, so I decided to go the library and do more research on Payton. After several days of doing that, I came across something he said that was the most profound thing I had ever heard. He was asked what makes him better than everyone else. He paused for a moment then said: "I want more than they do every day of the week." He added that, "in the off-season, when no one wants to run that dirt hill with me at six in the morning every day of the week, I want it more than they do. During the season on Monday, Tuesday, Wednesday, Thursday, Friday, and Saturday, when there are no fans in the stands and no cameras are rolling, I want it more than they do. Then on Sunday, I want it more than they do."

It's just what I needed as a young boy. I needed a mindset I could build on. And from that day on, when I practiced, when I trained, and when I played, I wanted it more than anyone else. That habit/mindset helped me get the most out of my god-given talents. No, I was never as good as Payton—not even close. But I got everything out of the talents I was given, and I live with peace knowing I did my part. I'm thankful for Payton and the mindset he shared because it impacted my life forever.

Tim Hughes

Tim Hughes is universally recognized as one of the world's leading pioneers and exponents of social selling and is currently ranked as the most influential social selling person in the world. He was responsible for a large-scale sales transformation within Oracle, the result of which delivered in excess of $100 million in sales uplift. He is currently leading a number of sales transformation programs in large business-to-business organizations. He is the co-founder and CEO of Digital Leadership Associates.

....

The person I want to give a standing O is Roger Turner.

Roger was a vice president at Oracle Corporation and my line manager. He was certainly the best manager I've had. Now, I've had a number of good managers—maybe I've been lucky—but like everybody, I've had some terrible managers, too. So what makes a good manager the Roger Turner way?

- **Making time.** Roger would book reviews with me, and it was my time. No interruptions, no "I've got to do this call." Sometimes he would ask questions, but otherwise it was my time to talk to him.

- **Asking the people digging the coal when you want to know how to mine it.** Many of the reviews would include him asking my advice on how best to run the team. He knew management can be a lonely place and can mean you become detached from the running of the business. Often the best ideas come from the people at the coal face. It didn't mean he would take my advice, but at least he could bring it into the mix.

- **Giving credit for ideas.** If you want to create a culture of idea creation, then you need to give credit for ideas provided by other people. I've had two managers since Roger, one of whom always gave credit for ideas that we put forward as a team—to the point that I sometimes thought he was being political. If the idea was rejected, he wouldn't lose political capital. But employees always shared their ideas. Another manager presented our ideas as his own, and we stopped putting them forward.

- **Believing in employees.** I always felt that Roger believed in me. If I asked for training, he supported me in it. He also sponsored me through the Oracle manager training.

- **Supporting career development.** Roger always insisted that we include training suggestions in any set of objectives. Some of his insistence might be due to the fact that he had worked at small companies and so knew the importance of training and access to it when you work for a big company. He also understood that a policy of constant learning was critical in today's business world. Let's not forget that once you climb to the top of one ladder, you are at the bottom of another ladder.

- **Delegating.** Probably one of the biggest issues that managers have is delegating responsibilities to other people. Often managers get used to simply telling people what to do because they think they know best, especially if they have worked their way up through the ranks. However, as a manager, you need to know that you don't have and cannot have all the good ideas. You need to be able to let your employees complete tasks themselves, make mistakes, and know that you will be there for them. Similar to children, they will climb trees, and they will either fall out of the tree or climb back down. Either way, you need to be there for them.

- **Doing what you say you will do and when you say you will do it.** One of the many mistakes managers have made over the years is saying they will do something and then not doing it. Often what they said they would do affected something I was planning to deliver around the same time. I would be unable to finish the project because I didn't have their contribution. We all have changing priorities and objectives, but when things change, it needs to be communicated.

- **Communicating often.** People want to know what is going on. Although all-hands calls and town hall meetings often sound dull, most employees want to understand the direction for an organization or department. What are the wins, what is the news, and have there been any changes? At the end of the day, you owe it to your people to offer them a stable, supportive environment—or, of course, they might leave.

As you can see, Roger taught me many things about management, and I hope you, too, can learn from his example.

Jesse Itzler

Jesse Itzler is the New York Times *bestselling author of* Living With a SEAL, *and* Living with The Monks. *He is a serial entrepreneur whose companies include Marquis Jet and Zico Coconut Water. When he is not running one-hundred-mile races, you can find him at the Atlanta Hawks games, where he is an owner of the team.*

....

When I was growing up, I wanted to be a professional basketball player. Scratch that, I wanted to be on the New York Knicks. The pursuit of that dream led to countless hours on the driveway. Every night I'd be out there, even after Mom turned off the floodlights. I'd imagine myself in double coverage and then I'd step back, spot up, and shoot it at the last second. The ball rotated in the air as the fans at Madison Square Garden looked on. And then the swish as the buzzzzzzer sounded. Itzler with the game-winning shot!

Well, after not making my high school basketball team, I realized the dream likely wouldn't happen. But the desire to be a professional athlete remained in my head. Maybe I could be a professional fencer? Squash? Bobsledding? Perhaps there was a sport that required less physical ability and more mental will. Or just something that required a relentless work ethic.

So in 2006 when I read there was no qualifying time needed to enter the USA Track and Field Ultramarathon Championship, I entered. That was my chance to be an elite athlete. I adjusted my goal from winning the race to completing one-hundred miles in less than twenty-four hours. I raised money during my training and received more than $1 million in donations, which increased the pressure to finish!

I gave myself ninety days to train. And I trained like a machine. I always tell people that when you have a BIG goal, the work necessary to accomplish it has to become an obsession. It has to become a part of your daily lifestyle and remain that way for the duration of the goal. With that mindset, I trained twice a day every day. That obsession carried over into the nights when I did extensive research, reading articles and watching videos about achieving goals. Most of what I found had the same five themes:

1. Have a specific date for your goal.
2. Have an accountability partner.
3. Put the goal in writing.
4. Have a detailed plan for accomplishing your goal.
5. Execute your plan.

The research helped me have a goal-oriented mindset, but ALL the knowledge went out the window at Mile 83. My ankles were swollen to the size of grapefruits, there were several toenails floating around in my socks, and blisters had appeared on my feet that looked like purple grapes you can find in the produce section at Whole Foods. I could have had my goal tattooed on my forehead and it wouldn't have helped me in that moment. F#ck those blogs and self-help videos about finishing what you start; they weren't going to run the last twenty-five miles.

As I wobbled back to the 1.1-mile dirt loop in Grapevine, Texas, I attempted to get back in the race. The short loop provided an opportunity to see the other runners during the race. And one of those runners was Pam Reed, a legend in the world of ultra-running. She's famous for not only completing the Badwater 135 (dubbed the world's toughest foot race), but winning it. As Pam passed me earlier in the race, we had started to chat. Well, as much as one can chat while running a hundred-mile race.

"I'm not feeling it today," she said. "This is my last lap. I'm going home." NO! I explained to Pam that I was running for charity and needed her help. I knew she could provide a wealth of information. She'd seen it all. I needed her with me for the balance of the race to "coach" me through the pain and guide me. She agreed with a smile and stuck with me for the duration of the race.

"Just keep moving," she said at Mile 83. "Block it out of your mind. It's not going to kill you. Keep moving forward. Don't stop."

It worked. I kept moving—one leg at a time, loop after loop.

"The pain will last a week," Pam said. "But you'll have the memory forever."

At Mile 89, she saw the self-doubt creeping back in. My legs were like Jell-O, and I truly wasn't sure I could finish. I wanted to quit. She looked me in the eye.

"No matter what," she said, "keep advancing. Do NOT sit down."

I crossed the finish line twenty-two hours and thirty minutes after the race started. It landed me in a wheelchair for three days, but I finished! I would never have made it without Pam's advice, guidance, and encouragement along the way. There are moments when we're faced with the decision to quit or keep going. But even those of us who choose to keep going sometimes are only willing to go 95 percent of the way. And yet it's that last 5 percent that is the difference between failure and amazing success and satisfaction.

Early on in any endeavor, we often ask people for advice. But very often we're seeking validation. As far as I know, validation has never helped complete a goal. Now when I need advice, I seek out people who can help move the needle. Forward. Keep advancing it. Pam was the expert I needed on one of the biggest days of my life.

Thanks, Pam.

Joe Jacobi

As America's first Olympic gold medalist in whitewater canoe slalom, Joe Jacobi promotes strategies and shares stories for living and performing at your best, doing the work that matters, and engaging with purpose. His platforms include performance coaching and training, professional speaking, broadcasting, and writing.

. . . .

A gust of Oklahoma wind ran right through to my bones. On a cold and gray Friday afternoon in November, I walked out of my office at the Oklahoma City Boathouse District for the final time.

I had built it up as my "dream job"—CEO of USA Canoe/Kayak, the national governing body for Olympic and Paralympic paddlesports in the United States. For five years, I had led the sport in which I and my doubles canoe partner, Scott Strausbaugh, won America's first ever Olympic gold medal in the sport of whitewater canoe slalom at the 1992 Olympic Games in Barcelona.

After a nineteen-year athletic career, I had shifted to coaching and then to being an NBC Olympic canoeing commentator before assuming the executive role at USA Canoe/Kayak. Leading the sport I love seemed like a natural next step.

High and low points marked an educational work and life experience at the organization. But after five years, I was ready for a change. On this final day in my job, I wasn't exactly sure into what I was changing.

Two days later, on Sunday morning, I opened my computer and started to write an email I would send to five friends. You know these kinds of emails, the ones you write just after leaving a job that conveys, "Hey, everything is good here." But really, it's not.

In this particular note, I went a little deeper than "please keep me in mind for..." and opened myself up to others in what felt like the first time in years. I shared a sense of positivity but also some fear, even vulnerability.

Their response? My friends said, "This is interesting. Write again next week."

So I did. I shared more thoughts about separating and transitioning from a sport that had been my identity for the previous thirty-plus years.

Their response? "Have you thought about sharing this with more people?"

Sunday Morning Joe was born.

My wife, Lisa, who owns a web development company, created a blog site for me, allowing friends and even strangers to read my posts and subscribe to receive them via my weekly email.

My inbox on Sunday mornings dramatically changed. My readership grew. Readers shared with me their perspective on my weekly topics, which covered life transitions, negative relationships, risks, small wins, and falling on your face. One of my popular posts was about literally falling on my face.

I found myself in conversations with people and on subjects I never could have imagined in my previous job. Somehow, the readers of *Sunday Morning Joe* and I were cutting through the noise, challenges, and resistance that sidetracked what matters in life in order to genuinely connect on a more purposeful level.

Every Sunday, I write the life message I need to hear for myself. But every Sunday, readers of *Sunday Morning Joe* take the experience to a much deeper level.

Their life changes and accomplishments facilitate self-reflection and investment that ultimately serve not only them, but their relationships, organizations, and communities.

As the readers improved their lives, they improved my life, too. For this, I gratefully stand and applaud our community of *Sunday Morning Joe* readers who make the start of the week a little bit better for all of us.

Phill Keene

Phill Keene is director of sales at Costello. Previously, he was director of marketing at Octiv and is the former co-host of the #RealSalesTalk *podcast. Keene brings commitment to learning and development to the inside sales space and was named one of 2017's top 25 most influential inside sales professionals by the American Association of Inside Sales Professionals. His expertise is in best practices around sales productivity, demand growth, lead generation, business development, and technology.*

....

When I think back on all the influences I have had that have gotten me to where I am today, there are a few specific people who come to mind: my high school football coach, a general manager from the time I spent in retail, my first business mentor I met while president of my fraternity at Ball State, and the CEO at my former employer. All those people have very specific moments I could look to and realize they got me through a pivotal point in my life and made me who I am today.

However, the person who has had the greatest impact on my life is my mother, Dorothy.

Growing up with her as a single mother, I watched her give everything she could to ensure that I had the best life she could possibly give me. She showed me what it was like to truly be selfless and care for other people. No matter how hard it was, she gave me more than I ever needed to be happy. Even when it felt like we would not have enough, somehow she found a way.

My mother was truly an inspiration to me, and I hope to share three things I learned from her.

The first thing she showed me is that you can give everything you have to other people without expecting anything else in return.

Throughout my youth and teenage years, my mother worked full-time and did what she could to take care of my brother and me. That whole time, she never missed any of my sports games or plays and always had something special planned for my birthday. No matter what it was, she was there.

Every year on the first day of school, she found a way to get me a new pair of shoes. She probably spent the last dollar in the account or picked up extra hours more times than I was aware of to make sure I had a new baseball mitt or cleats for football. I cannot even begin to imagine the stress she likely faced when times were tough.

No matter what my brother or I needed, she did it and never complained. The second thing I learned from my mother is to push yourself out of your comfort zone and give it everything you have.

There were a few times I can recall having conversations with my mother about things going on in her life that were new to her or that made her uncomfortable. I cannot remember her ever backing down from a challenge.

For six years during the full-time work, games, and events, she would go to college at night and do homework, even on the nights when she had to go to a baseball game a few towns over. I still have no idea how, but she made it work.

In those six years, I could not even begin to tell you the number of times she took a 400-level class that was a bit out of her wheelhouse, which usually led to her spending hours with her head down in a book studying, then coming home convinced that she had performed poorly on a test only to find out that she'd gotten an A.

That is how she handles everything in life. When something gets thrown at her, she gives it everything she has and does not back down even though it might make her uncomfortable. She puts her head down, figures it out to the best of her ability, and gets an A.

The third thing I learned from my mother is the importance of family.

She grew up one of fifteen children, and being around family was a major part of growing up. I was fortunate enough from a young age to have family be at the center of my life.

My mother was able to show me that family members are supposed to have your back. When things were hard, her brothers and sisters stepped up, and no matter what time of the day or night, when someone in her family needed something, my mother was there, no questions asked. She just showed up.

There are times in life when things go in a different direction than you intended them to, but when you give them everything you have, your family can be a rock to lean on. My mother was the rock, and even when I did not turn to her for help, I knew she would be there anyway. I never felt alone.

My mother is a driving force that pushed me to make her proud and get where I am today. I can never do enough to repay all the time, effort, money, and love she has given me. I am truly grateful.

Anne Kubitsky

Anne Kubitsky is a social entrepreneur, author/illustrator, and founder of the Look for the Good Project, a nonprofit that helps kids uplift their schools with gratitude and kindness. Kubitsky's first book, What Makes You Grateful?, *was featured on MSNBC, in* Reader's Digest, *and in* The Huffington Post. *Her latest book,* Together We Rise, *is a collaboration of people from all over the world to help fund her scholarship program.* Opening to Good *is a picture book recounting her journey from marine biology to art and the development of the Look for the Good Project.*

....

I met Dave Lutian in November, about three years after I started the Look for the Good Project. We were standing outside a church, shivering in our boots, as he painstakingly gave me directions. A few weeks later, he sat at my kitchen table, wide-eyed, as I poured out my soul, telling him all the reasons he should leave. Death, betrayal, rape, codependency—these were just a few of the things I was grappling with when I met Dave. Even though I barely knew him, the painful memories oozed out of me, making the air so thick I could barely breathe.

"Why was he still here?" I wondered. "As the founder of the Look for the Good Project, I'm supposed to embody gratitude and a positive mindset. He must be so disappointed. Surely I'll never see him after this!" Unfazed, he returned smiling the next day, laden with food and an offer to shovel my snowy driveway.

Our conversations grew and so did our friendship. Dave had just been offered a new job and asked for my advice. Even though I wanted him to stay in Connecticut, I encouraged him to follow his heart to Philadelphia for this special career opportunity. Dave left, and we continued to keep in touch. By March, he told me he'd show up for me no matter what, even if it meant driving three hours out of his way simply to buy me groceries. "You're family," he said as he paid the cashier.

Although I loved my job, I wasn't proud of the financial position I was in. The Look for the Good Project had recently reorganized into a non-profit organization, and I was attempting to scrape by on a poverty-level stipend, working 80 hours a week to keep everything going. I developed a school bullying prevention program, reworked the website, designed books, organized fundraising efforts, held board meetings, managed volunteers, traveled to schools, forged essential partnerships for the non-profit, and racked up the credit card debt. My parents lived just down the road and offered free food and the use of their car, so I thought it was safe to bootstrap the startup for at least a little longer. But like a sailor in a small boat being tossed at sea, I was quickly losing my bearings.

By April, the storm hit. My parents could no longer afford my childhood home and needed to relocate to another area of the country. They put the house up for sale, and it sold within a week.

My birthday was spent amid a flurry of loud voices, clutter, and boxes. Overwhelmed with the thirty years of stuff they had accumulated, my parents began throwing out photographs, heirlooms, and other things that were important to me. In an attempt to salvage these family treasures and relocate to a more permanent address, I quickly found a studio in a rough neighborhood about an hour north. Dave called often and drove up every weekend, even getting his friends to help me move.

By June, Dave had transferred back to Connecticut to be closer to me, my parents had moved far away, and the stress of trying to keep myself afloat had finally crept into my body. A lump had formed, and the doctor thought it was cancerous. I found a surgeon; Dave paid for the procedure.

By October, the stress had crept into my mind, and I was prescribed an anti-anxiety medication "just in case." Dave held my hand and let me cry on his shoulder. As the tears streamed down, I suddenly remembered the location where I had been sexually assaulted as a teen. In my haste to move, I hadn't realized that I had relocated to the town of the crime and had been driving by the exact location twice a week since I'd moved. Dave held me while I sobbed. "It's OK," he assured me. In these moments, Dave chose to wholeheartedly accept and love me *just as I was.* I didn't have to put up a front. I was just me, and he loved me for that very reason. His kindness gave me permission to remember the experiences I had suppressed, grieve over the people I had lost, and actively rebuild my life. Since we met, Dave has supported me with astounding generosity. He has donated thousands of dollars to the Look for the Good Project and personally subsidized my efforts to restructure the organization.

In just two years, our school program has reached 67,000 children in nineteen states who have written over one million messages of gratitude. The program has also been endorsed by the Connecticut commissioner of education and the Connecticut Association of Schools and is even helping schools gain national recognition through the U.S. Department of Education.

My standing O goes to Dave Lutian for never giving up on me and for making so many sacrifices to develop the Look for the Good Project and support the next generation of student leaders through our school program. To learn more about our program, please visit lookforthegoodproject.org.

Jenn Kuehn

Jenn Kuehn is a successful entrepreneur, philanthropist, motivational speaker, fitness guru, life strategist, and single mom. She founded SHiFT Cycling and Balance in 2013. Her mission is to continually impact the lives of others. She articulates her generosity by working with numerous nonprofit groups, including the Sarah Foundation, Haiti180, Girl Up, and Crohn's and Colitis Foundation.

People often ask me if I'm always happy. When you see me, more often than not I've got a smile on my face and I'm looking to spread my positive vibes. But that wasn't always the case.

I didn't realize the powerful impact that positivity can have until I met Professor Tara Stuart. She was my inspiration back in 1997 at Keene State College. Let's remember that back in the 1990s, mindfulness, positivity, and happiness weren't even considered. I was studying communications, and when I walked into her class, I didn't know the long-term impact she would have on me. Professor Stuart has the voice of an angel, and when she spoke, we listened. She has a unique ability to get an entire group involved in a discussion about happiness and whether we create it or earn it.

As part of the course, we had to read *Living, Loving and Learning* by Leo Buscaglia. It was in those pages that I began to see life differently. Buscaglia was a pioneer in living a life of love, saying, "Life is our greatest possession and love its greatest affirmation."

I've always been a positive, upbeat, high-energy person. That energy has power. Professor Stuart challenged us to understand the power of our energies and use them to create a positive, happy life. I learned that happiness is a choice. For the next twenty-plus years, I have evolved and strengthened my knowledge and commitment to spreading happiness to others. I built SHiFT Cycling and Balance, a company with a core mission and purpose to create a happy experience.

It's not something you can buy. It's not a trait you inherit. Contrary to what some might think or say, happiness is not a status you achieve or a destination you reach. At some point in our lives, we (myself included) have chased happiness, fiercely determined to check the box that says, "YES! I am happy!" But happiness isn't a box you check, an item you cross off a list, a material item for sale, or a status. Happiness is a choice.

It's like the sun: You can't look at it directly, but when you look at it indirectly, you feel it. Don't confront it face to face; instead, approach it from a different angle. Take a step back and focus your time and energy on the things that excite you. Find significance and meaning in what you do. When you're able to feel that, you'll discover your true self, your purpose, and your true happiness. After all, without significance, purpose, and meaning, what's the point?

It's more than a choice. It's a mindset. And it affects every aspect of your life.

Choose happy.

Your mindset impacts your choices. When you are in a positive mindset, you make better decisions. You eat better, get to bed earlier, exercise, meditate, and make time for you. On the flip side, when we're struggling, we tend to resort to vices to cope with our unhappiness. What are the negative habits you resort to when you're in a bad place? Some of us withdraw from others, overeat, stay in bed, consume adult beverages, etc. You have the power to choose your mindset.

Every day isn't going to be filled with sunshine and sunflowers. Pain is inevitable; it's part of life and it's where we grow. But suffering through it is optional. Each time we experience pain, we increase our capacity for joy. When you acknowledge that the situations and obstacles you face are tough but choose to make the best of the situation, you are choosing happy. Focus on the strength you are gaining through the adversity.

Make a commitment to choose happy.

- Live a week of creating more happiness and less misery.
- Send a friend a note saying you are grateful for him or her.
- Smile! Happiness is the choice to smile in the face of adversity.

Jaime Lannon Diglio

Jaime Lannon Diglio is president and founder of InFirst. She previously held sales leadership roles at Microsoft and Gartner. She has advised hundreds of organizations on how to lift culture, shift mindsets, and leverage technology to take people and revenue to the next level. She built a $40 million business in a new market from the ground up, and specializes in turning average teams into growth engines. She is dedicated to work alongside leaders who know that tapping into the power of people is the key to winning the war on talent, driving innovation, shifting culture, and increasing revenue.

. . . .

I've been blessed by having two people in my life who have supported me, helped me choose courage over comfort, and prompted me to develop a leadership philosophy centered around being myself and seeing the impact of investing in people.

The first is my mom, the most courageous person I know.

From a young age, I remember my parents struggling to pay the bills. Then when I was seven, my sister was five, and my brother was two, my dad became ill. I remember my mom being incredibly stressed about having to take care of three young children and a sick husband. Our family was unable to make ends meet on the money she was earning managing a laboratory for a local medical center. She even ran a sewing business on the side, but the two incomes still were not enough.

So she dug deep and thought big: If she could operate one facility's lab well, why not multiple medical center laboratories? She enrolled in a master's program and started her own firm—South Shore Laboratory Consultants Inc. Thirty years later, her company is advising some of the largest and most prestigious medical facilities in Boston and across the U.S.

Throughout her struggle, she chose courage. Courage to move forward and take a risk to provide for us. Courage to change the outcome for herself and our family. Her example has left a lasting impression on me and convinced me that courage has the power to change the world. Again and again, I've witnessed how one person's courage can send a ripple throughout communities and across generations.

By believing in herself, my mom taught me that I could be anything I wanted to be, and she has nurtured that belief through every stage of my life. Her courage taught me to BELIEVE.

The second is my husband, the most empowering person I know.

Matt grew up in a family of teachers, coaches, and runners. He ran for Duke University and graduated with an ambition to do something other than teaching. Despite what he thought he wanted, he had a natural calling and became a high school teacher and cross-country coach.

When my husband started coaching at a small school in Connecticut, he didn't even have enough kids to field a team. Over the last ten years, he's poured countless hours into molding his boys and girls into top cross-country teams in New England. Today, his team is larger than any other sport in the school.

Each year, at the end of the season, he asks each of the seniors to give a speech. At the end of last season, one of his captains said: "Coach, you've taught me that potential lies at the end of a long and winding road. You've taught me to be persistent and not intimidated by adversity. You've taught me lessons that I can carry for the rest of my life. I look up to you, and I thank you for making me into the person I am today."

He has built a following. A community within a community. My husband's quiet leadership philosophy has taught his "kids" that humility is empowering. By keeping the focus on the students, not himself, he has done more than build a team, he has created a lifelong ripple effect that impacts the lives of countless kids and their families.

If there is anything I can leave you with, it's the wisdom I've gained from my journey.

My mom and my husband have given me the courage to be me and to follow my true passion for empowering others to believe in themselves. From my mother and my husband, I leave you with these inspiring messages:

- Be grateful for what you have today and use that gratitude to aim at what you want for the future.
- When you see something amazing in other people, tell them. Your positive words could change their lives.
- Always leave people better than how you found them. Focus on growing the good.
- Surround yourself with people who make you want to be the best version of yourself.

Scott Leese

Scott Leese is one of the top startup sales leaders in the country. Through domestic and international consulting, he has trained an army of salespeople that is thousands strong. Leese puts his more than thirteen years of sales and leadership experience to use as the founder of Scott Leese Consulting LLC and SurfandSales.com and as senior vice president of sales at Qualia Labs Inc. A highly sought-after consultant, advisor, leader, and trainer, Leese has a proven record of success building sales teams from the ground up.

....

Many of us can point to a specific person who has been influential in shaping our lives and our relative success. I can certainly come up with an enormous and well-deserving list of parents, friends, colleagues, teachers, and coaches. But there is one person in my life who truly deserves a standing O.

My grandmother, Antonina DiGregorio, came from a Sicilian family that immigrated to Brooklyn and later to Buffalo and Niagara Falls, New York. She is now in her mid-nineties and would be slightly mortified if I shared her family history, so I am mindful of respecting her privacy.

She was the rock of her entire family from a very young age and has remained a pillar of strength, service, kindness, and humility her entire life. She was a second mother to my brother and me and to a number of our friends. She never asked for a thing but gave willingly through her time, energy, and impact on others.

In my early twenties, I experienced a prolonged period of illness that nearly took my life and forever altered it. There is one moment I will never forget with her during this experience. It happened during a brief week or two when I was not hospitalized and was trying to convalesce at home. However, I relapsed. I was re-hospitalized and headed for surgeries. The struggle would go on another few years, but that is not the point of the story.

Pumped full of narcotics for pain, an immunosuppressant, and steroid medication designed to reduce inflammation, I was an insomniac with uncontrollable rage and a mind bordering on madness. It is very lonely when you're sick as hell and it's 3 a.m. and you cannot sleep. You eventually lose track of the normalcy of time and space. So, of course, I called my grandmother in the middle of the night because I knew that she often had trouble sleeping and was a very early riser.

She answered the phone sounding terribly groggy and half-asleep (as she should at 3 a.m.!). I told her I was not doing well and was going to try to walk my dog over to her house about a mile away from mine. This was not a smart move because I was far too weak to make it around the block, let alone a mile away. Her response was: "Wait there. I will come to you." She was in her mid-seventies at the time. She didn't think twice about walking a mile alone at 3 a.m. to come help me fight my battle both physically and mentally.

We went on a walk together and talked—well, mostly I talked because I was a rambling mess desperate for relief and healing. She listened. I remember wondering at the time if I would ever be capable of the amount of empathy and concern she had for me. I had always thought of myself as invincible, and here I was at one of my lowest lows, finally learning that it wasn't all about me. A hard lesson but a vital one to learn. She told me to keep fighting. She told me of her secret past and how impossibly hard it had been at times and why she kept going. She helped give me the strength I need to never give up and showed me that real love, real family, and real friendship will be there when you have nothing to offer up yourself. They are simply there to keep you going.

Grandma, you deserve a standing O for all you have done—not just for me but for so many others.

Take a bow.

Larry Levine

During his thirty years of sales experience, Larry Levine has sold office technology, document management, and managed services to customers ranging from small businesses to Fortune 500 companies. In 2013, he became an account rep for a Japanese manufacturer in Los Angeles, one of the most competitive markets in the United States. Using the foundation of LinkedIn, his social strategies, and his sales strategies, he booked more than $1.3 million in new sales in 2014 and left a $1.6 million pipeline. Levine now coaches and inspires sales leaders and their teams to do what he did, and is the author of Selling from the Heart.

....

Nothing brings about success like walking through the right doors.

Those who are close to me, and know the real me, know I have no problem asking for help. It is not a sign of weakness. It is an opportunity to expand your horizons. I'm flabbergasted by the amount of people who simply fail to ask for help.

I've made it my mission to educate, engage, and excite all those inside the sales world. Sales leaders and their teams must stand up, unite, and transform how they go to market in a world full of sales sameness.

Who are you, and what makes you different from others?

I believe every sales rep must articulate a strong value proposition and tailor it to different stakeholders. They must devote a tremendous amount of effort to understanding customers, their needs, their wants, and their issues and packaging all of this up by focusing on adding value every step of the way.

I spent twenty-seven years inside an extremely old-school sales channel, laggard in nature and slow to adapt to modern ways of growing business: the copier channel. I've directed many pointed blogs at the industry. I speak loudly about how copier sales reps must transform themselves. They must take it upon themselves to be innovative inside a very slow-to-adapt sales channel.

I now direct this same message to every sales channel out there. How are you innovating? How are you adapting to what is happening around you? What's standing in your way?

Evolve or Face the Consequences

In life, stuff happens. In spring 2015, I found myself in a position where life took a massive turn. We all face challenging times in life. We can either let it consume us as we fade into a downward life spiral or we can use it as a launching pad to reinvent, reinvigorate, and reignite passion—a passion to challenge one's mindset and skill set to start something new.

I've had the fortunate experience of meeting many amazing people throughout my lifetime. With a massive amount of gratitude, my standing ovation and heartfelt thanks go to someone who believed in me—my dear friend Darrell Amy. Without a doubt, he is the most genuine, authentic, and caring individual I know. His belief in me and, more important, his ability to push me out of my comfort zone have changed me for the better, and I am forever grateful!

I wish to publicly recognize and say thank you to Darrell Amy. I learned more about myself from this man, and without his friendship, encouragement, and daily inspiration, I would not be doing what I'm doing now.

The Launch of Something Special

Evolve or perish—two words being thrown at sales reps all over the world. Evolve to me means trying something new, adapting, adopting, and constantly being on the lookout to improve everything about what you do.

With the utmost support from Darrell Amy, my business baby was launched to the sales world. The Social Sales Academy is fully committed to helping business-to-business sales teams integrate social into their sales process to ignite and fuel sales growth. We want you to get results. We're passionate about doing this the right way, the genuine way, the authentic way. Straight from the heart!

Creating Visibility

How do you expect to get noticed in a marketplace when nobody knows you exist?

In a highly digital business world, how do salespeople get noticed? How do they rise above all others to stand out?

You have to be willing to put yourself out there. Integrating social is jet fuel to anybody in sales who uses it in conjunction with every other prospecting strategy. I threw myself out into the marketplace to get noticed, combined with a strict work ethic. I leveraged outbound strategies coupled with a commitment to social and marketed what I was all about inside the sales channel I grew up in—the copier channel.

I pounded the phone. I drove emails. I spoke at industry events. I wrote articles in industry magazines. I started blogging. I leveraged every single business development tool available to get noticed. I made this a non-negotiable deal. In the span of two years, I've written more than 135 blog posts and more than forty published articles, and I have spoken at events all over the United States, Canada, and Australia.

I've worked with sales leaders and their teams throughout the United States, Australia, and Canada. I've created excitement and proof that social integrated into the sales process does work. I like to consider myself the biggest excuse-remover out there.

I'm in the process of publishing my first book, *Selling From the Heart: How Your Authentic Self Sells You* (to be released by summer 2018).

I share this with all of you because you have the capability to make this happen for you. We've all been given the same sets of tools to use. It's how we choose to use them. The commitment I made to myself matters the most. My personal goal and commitment: I want to make a difference by helping salespeople become the sales professionals I know they can become.

Selling From the Heart Podcast and Jeb Blount

In April 2017, the *Selling From the Heart* podcast was born. This was another avenue for Darrell and me to get our message out to the sales world. Our podcast is all about being genuine, being real, being authentic, and speaking from the heart as we help the sales community all over the world.

The guests who come onto our podcast share our same mission and are advocates of selling from the heart.

One podcast guest changed my world: Jeb Blount, CEO of Sales Gravy.

As the author of Sales EQ, Jeb shared his research into curiosity as a core sales skill on our podcast. Here's where it takes a turn. Later that evening, I heard my cell phone ringing. I didn't recognize the number and almost didn't answer, but I did.

"Hey, Larry, it's Jeb. Just wanted to call to say thank you again for having me on the podcast." I'm saying to myself, "Holy crap!" For the next hour and a half, we had a phenomenal conversation. The turning point came when Jeb mentioned that in April 2018, he, Mark Hunter, Mike Weinberg, and Anthony Iannarino were putting on the Outbound Sales Conference.

Jeb said, "I've been following what you've been doing and what you've been writing about, and I like what you stand for. Would you like to share your story, your journey, and how you have tied outbound with social strategies to get where you are and speak at Outbound?" Oh my freaking bleep, bleep, bleep. "Hell yeah, Jeb, I would be honored!"

Let me tell you this: If you never put yourself out there, how do you plan on getting noticed? How do you plan on attracting new sales opportunities? How do you plan on rising above all your competitors? Become comfortable with who you are. Share the real you and not some facade in the hope that it will impress others and help you get noticed. The path I chose and carved out for myself has been done my way. The authentic way, the genuine way, the human way by staying real and being real by saying things that need to be said.

People will see, smell, and sense B.S. a mile away. If you can't be the real you, then who are you?

My Story, My Way, The Way I Know How

I share this with you for one reason and one reason only: You all have the ability to change your lives. It requires believing in yourself, staying true to yourself, and not letting the voices of others take you down.

We all have stories to tell. We all have a voice, and the message needs to be told in your unique way as you help change the lives of those around you.

I encourage every sales leader and every sales professional to create a plan. This plan revolves around and encompasses leveraging every single business development tool available to help you get noticed in a crowded marketplace. Think of your current clients, your future clients, your network, your inner circle, and your fellow teammates. How can you help them become better versions of themselves? How can you help them all in doing better business?

I know you have it in you. If a fifty-three-year-old guy can reinvent and repackage himself, then I believe you can do it. Trust me—it will change your life! I'm having the time of my life. I wish the same for you.

I hope this inspires you to take action. You owe it to yourself, your career, and your family.

You owe it to yourself to be yourself!

Brad Mason

Brad Mason is a lawyer, a leader with a financial services technology company, a board member of an inner-city youth group, and founder and head coach of The Give Team, the only inner-city obstacle course racing team in the country with a focus on goal setting and leadership skills. The Give Team's motto is "No matter how little you have, you always have something to give. BE STRONG! GIVE MORE!" He received his law degree from Drake University and is a graduate of the University of Connecticut.

. . . .

When I was a cornerback, pads were weapons. Designed to protect, they also caused harm, and I intended to inflict pain on anyone in my way. Midway through the season, it was my first practice at my new school, and I had a chip on my shoulder. In nearly every drill, I blew through teammates. I had little patience and low tolerance for everything except pain. Although I was performing well, I didn't want to be there. I hadn't wanted to move across the country. I wanted to be back in Spokane with my friends, my girlfriend, and my real football team, and I was taking it out on anyone in front of me.

After the season ended, I sought out Coach Larry Ciotti. We needed to talk. I was quitting. The challenges of moving to a new town were difficult on a fragile adolescent psyche. The team I had left behind in Spokane played for the state championship and lost. The team I joined played for the state championship and won. But that championship didn't feel like mine. I had crashed a party.

I heard the door to the locker room open and felt the strong presence of Coach Ciotti enter the room. I hadn't known him long, but I respected him. He had started the football program at Daniel Hand High School in 1970, and it became a Connecticut powerhouse with five state titles and an unrivaled winning tradition. I sat nervously in his office. I don't remember what we said, but there was no pressure from him to stay on the team. If I wanted to quit, I could quit.

Nearly a year later, I sought out Coach again. I sat excitedly in the same chair. I had a question. Did he think I could play college football? The day before, I'd received an honorable mention in the New Haven Register All-State Football Team.

What happened between January and December 1985? Larry Ciotti's coaching philosophy brought out much of what my family instilled in me but at a time and in a way nobody else was capable of doing. He turned an undersized, apathetic football player from a quitter into a member of the all state football team. He turned a kid who never even considered playing college football into a Hand football alumnus who was confident he could compete on the field with anyone.

Coach Ciotti focused on hard work, effort, conditioning, and learning by action. Practice was designed to be four times harder than games. Although Ciotti inherited good players over the years, Hand teams were regularly undersized and often less talented than the competition. You can't control talent, but you can control effort and conditioning. As a result, work ethic and preparation were at the heart of Ciotti's championship heritage. Ciotti-coached teams were in better condition. If the game was decided in the fourth quarter, Hand would win. Coach likes to say if we lost a game, it was because we ran out of time.

These principles instilled in me by Coach Larry Ciotti are brought forward every day as I serve my community.

In 2016, I started an inner-city obstacle course racing team called The Give Team based in a neighborhood named one of America's most dangerous. We gather every Saturday morning at 7 a.m. for an intense workout, then meet over breakfast to discuss goals and a weekly topic on leadership. At the end of every season, we compete in an obstacle course race.

The standards carried forward to The Give Team from Hand football are as follows:

- The Give Team motto is "No matter how little you have, you always have something to give. BE STRONG! GIVE MORE!"
- Our team doesn't avoid obstacles. We seek them out and conquer them.
- We seek pain because it's the pain you seek that strengthens you, preparing you for the pain life inevitably throws at you.
- My job as coach isn't to create happiness or contentment. My job is to build strength. With strength, team members will find their own happiness and contentment. Absent strength, any happiness and contentment will be fleeting.

As a result of the values from Coach Ciotti, Give Team members are on a path to achieving great things. One is the youngest member of the Ph.D. program in computer science at Auburn University. Another has earned a full academic scholarship to the University of Florida and is walking onto the track team.

For that, I give Coach Larry Ciotti a standing O.

Matthew McDarby

Matthew McDarby is the author of The Cadence of Excellence: Key Habits of Effective Sales Managers *and managing director of Specialized Sales Systems. He is the founder of United Sales Resources and a former vice president of enterprise sales at Huthwaite, one of the world's leading sales training companies and creator of SPIN Selling. McDarby has coached and advised hundreds of sales leaders and their teams in a wide range of industries, helping them win new business and create value for their clients.*

....

I owe my father such an enormous debt that it would be a missed opportunity to write about anyone else. Dad's is a story of overcoming huge disadvantages by sticking to some basic principles: Tell the truth. Do what you said you would do. Treat others with respect.

To understand John McDarby's story, it is important to go back a couple of generations before him. His grandfather, Edward, was killed in a farming accident in 1890 in Ireland. Edward left a young wife, Margaret, and four children, all of whom were sent off to the Athy Workhouse because they had no other means to financially take care of themselves. Young Edward (known as Ned), the youngest of the four children, was sent to work as a stable hand at the nearby Crosby estate. He worked there for a few years until he decided to leave Ireland and board a ship bound for New York and a better life.

Ned's was a typical Irish immigrant's story. He found work as a motorman in the railroad, and his work ethic made it possible to generate a sufficient income for his young wife, Helen, and their growing family. Helen had been a housekeeper for a wealthy family in Liverpool before she chased Ned across the Atlantic to keep him for herself. (That's a story for another book.) Ned and Helen married and settled their young family in the South Bronx.

Ned was a hardworking, decent man who was deeply devoted to his wife and children. My dad was Ned's youngest son. He was born in 1928 and lived a fairly typical Bronx Irish Catholic life with his five sisters and two brothers. Each one of the McDarby children learned the value of hard work and honesty from the example of their two wonderful parents.

In the dark, early hours of a September morning in 1934, Ned was walking to work when he was struck and killed by a hit-and-run driver. The McDarby family of 286 East 156th Street was without its primary breadwinner, and young Johnny, only five years old, lost his father before he could really get to know him. And so, as was typical of Irish-American families at that time, Helen, Johnny, and the other McDarbys pulled their lives together the best they could. They would carry on Ned's legacy by virtue of their hard work, their integrity, and their honesty. Johnny witnessed his oldest siblings go off to serve their country in war or work to help take care of the family's needs, sacrificing their teenage years and having to forgo what other kids had in order to do what was right. Johnny learned from their example as well.

From a very young age, I can remember my father emphasizing how important it was to tell the truth. Looking back now, I realize it might have been one of the few important lessons that his father, Ned, had the chance to pass on to him before dying. I imagine that might have been one of the few lessons that Ned's father passed along to him before he, too, passed away tragically.

Telling the truth served Dad well throughout his professional career. His reputation in business was an honorable one. He could be counted on to do what he said he would do. John McDarby's integrity was his business card, the only one he would ever really need as he navigated the corporate world from the 1950s to 1980s. My sister, Anne, observed, "Dad never felt entirely comfortable in that world, but one thing that is certain is he couldn't help but be himself. He just wasn't able to put on a false face."

His reputation and hard work carried him to the level of executive vice president, leading sales teams in one of the toughest places in the country to compete and win in the commercial property and casualty insurance business. Dad took good care of his customers, and his colleagues and staff showed him the utmost respect. Later in his career, his colleagues labeled his sales team "John's Army," a nod to his military service in the Korean War and also his great discipline, integrity, and work ethic.

Dad and I talked only a little bit about my career in sales and sales leadership before he passed away in 2007, but he was particularly pleased to hear stories about my successes. He encouraged me to put my absolute best effort into all that I did, but he always emphasized that success could not come at the expense of my integrity. He knew intuitively that building trust—a critical skill in what I do professionally—depends entirely on being honest and doing what you said you would do. If I have any superpowers as a seller, that one comes straight from Dad.

He also taught me and my siblings to avoid thinking we are better than anyone else. Everyone has a story, and everyone knows something I don't, regardless of their station in life or where they fit on an organizational chart. That is what makes it possible for me to communicate with a CEO, a janitor, or a middle manager like a peer. I try to demonstrate to my children how important it is to treat everyone with respect, and in their own way, they live out Grandpa John's example, showing kindness and respect to those who might not otherwise get much of either.

In a profession where the desire to win tempts one to play fast and loose with facts, I have the constant reminder of John McDarby's looming words: Tell the truth. There is no other way. I am most proud, above any accomplishments I might have, that my children understand what it means to be John McDarby's grandkids. Thank you, Dad, for your example and what it means to my family every day.

West McDonald

West McDonald is vice president of business development at Print Audit and owner of FocusMPS. He has a ton of fun in the office equipment and managed services channels and has been recognized as one of the top 40 most influential people in the imaging industry in 2013 and ENX Difference Maker in 2015 and 2017. Outside of work he is a die-hard Star Wars *fan, family man, mountain biker, kayak enthusiast, and all-around nerd who is happily caught in a business person's body.*

....

The first time I saw *Star Wars*, I was seven years old and the year was 1977. At that time, I lived in a small prairie town with a population of fewer than 1,000 people. Coming away from watching that movie, I felt like a young Luke Skywalker and knew that one day I, too, would find adventure and excitement in a place far, far away.

Fast-forward to today and my life is very different. I own my own business, I am the vice president for an incredible software company, and I have had more professional and personal adventures than I could have ever imagined or dreamed possible back then. The tenets of that space opera have remained an indelible Force within my life and have acted as a guiding hand for where I am today, both personally and professionally. George Lucas, thank you!

My standing O isn't for George, however. It is for somebody in my professional and adult life who has shown me in practice what *Star Wars* showed me on the big screen as a child. My standing O is going out to the most George Lucas-like person I know today: John MacInnes.

Allow me to elaborate on why he deserves a standing O for three reasons by using three of my favorite *Star Wars* quotes:

- **"Do or do not. There is no try."** Those are my favorite words of any in the *Star Wars* films. Although spoken by Yoda, they were written by George Lucas, and he lived those words to the core. When he embarked on the first *Star Wars* film, nobody believed he would succeed, but he did—beyond anybody's wildest imaginings.

Like Lucas, John MacInnes is a doer. He is a serial and fearless entrepreneur. When he gets a great idea, he takes action and makes it into a vibrant reality. He doesn't try; he just does. He also supports other people in doing. I've become more of a doer myself by learning from his example and through his patient tutelage.

- **"Never tell me the odds!"** Han Solo yelled this line at C-3PO when they were about to fly into an asteroid field, right after C-3PO told Han that the odds of successfully navigating an asteroid field were approximately 3,720 to 1. One thing that John has taught me is that if you are going to advance in your life or career, you need to be fearless and willing to work harder than the next person to achieve success. The odds don't matter, only the attitude and actions reflective of winning. I've seen him beat the odds on more occasions than I can list in this short essay. I have learned to win more and try less thanks to his daily examples of the same.

- **"The Force will be with you. Always."** These were the last mortal words spoken by Ben Kenobi to Luke Skywalker. Shortly after this, Ben was cut down by Darth Vader in an iconic lightsaber duel. He sacrificed himself not for fame or pride but rather out of a genuine desire to help others.

There have been times when I've needed somebody to have my back, both personally and professionally, and without fail, the first person to step up to the plate has always been John MacInnes. I've seen him do it for plenty of other people, too. In every single case, he helped not because of obligation but because of a genuine desire to do the right thing.

I've seen him volunteer time to help young entrepreneurs strengthen their approach to business. I've seen John jump in to make personal difficulties easier for people when they need the help the most. I've yet to meet any other business leader who takes such genuine interest in supporting the well-being and growth of the people he works with. He does all this without seeking accolades or a pat on the back. John helps people because he genuinely believes that people matter more than anything else. His sense of charity and genuine concern and his willingness to make a difference are the primary reasons I'm giving him this standing O.

With John, you see, it's less about how strong the Force is with him but rather how he helps others become stronger with it. He inspires and supports those who are lucky enough to work with him. John leads by example and has an uncanny knack for keeping people motivated and working toward a common cause. Most important, John gives freely of himself and his time for the benefit of others.

George Lucas and John MacInnes would certainly get along well if they ever crossed paths. The Force, after all, is very strong with them both.

Roll credits.

Marc Megna

Marc Megna has evolved into the foremost strength and conditioning coach in Miami. The former NFL football player is certified by the National Strength and Conditioning Association and has years of experience in this field. He is a sponsored strength and conditioning coach for Iovate Health Sciences and endorses their Muscletech supplement line. Megna writes about fitness, exercises, and training tips for Muscle & Fitness, Inside Fitness, Fitness RX, Train Magazine, Dr. Oz, *and* Elitefts.com.

. . . .

I'm just a guy from Fall River, Massachusetts. I didn't have a privileged childhood, but I definitely had a huge advantage, a secret weapon of sorts. I had a mother with heart and courage. She taught me the most important lessons in life. She told me to dream big and never quit. She said I should acknowledge the fault, take responsibility, and improve, but never, ever quit. When I'm tired, I think of her. When my motivation weakens, I think of her.

There were times when I thought I knew it all and thought I would do a better job than the people for whom I previously worked. It's like being a sports fan and calling "better" plays from your couch. You don't know what it's like until you're there on the field—or for me, until I decided that I would pursue my dream of starting my own business. It took me three decades, but I did it.

My mom raised my brother and me while working insane hours and never complaining. We had a little apartment and spent tons of time together. She was my hero. I really don't know how she did it.

My mother instilled in me that hard work and a caring heart trump all, but never allow yourself to be bullied. Don't aim to be liked by all; instead, aim to be respected. You can have it, but you must earn it.

When building my team, I remembered my mother's lessons about working hard and having a caring heart. Choose teammates (in business or on the field) who have high character, can communicate well, and have pure hearts. You're not looking for the BEST ones, you're looking for the RIGHT ones. You've invested your blood, sweat, and yes, tears, into your dream. But when things go well, it will ultimately be because of the team.

My mother left us many years ago. I miss her like crazy. My life goal is to make her proud. If I can someday be half of what she was, I'll be hugely fulfilled. Her spirit lives inside me, and I will share it with the world. Thank you for teaching me to be kind and mindful of others. Love you, Mom. Here is my standing O to you.

Always ROASTL! Thx for your support,
♡, Katharine

Katherine Voyles Mobley

Katharine Voyles Mobley is an award-winning marketer with a proven track record of driving revenue growth for global brands and technology startups. She is the CMO for First Advantage, a global background screening company with twenty-six locations and 4,000 employees worldwide. Throughout her twenty-year tenure as a marketer, she has been dedicated to blazing a trail for the next generation of women in technology and is a respected Woman in Technology. Since 2016, she has served as a formal mentor for residents of the Atlanta Tech Village, the fourth largest startup incubator in the world.

. . . .

The word "influence" by definition is the capacity to have an effect on the character, development, or behavior of someone or something. As I reflect on my professional life and those who helped me get where I am today, I have to go back to one person who has had one of the greatest positive influences on my life, during one of the most challenging times.

In 1989, I found myself living with multiple families as I attempted to get through high school and get myself into college. My parent's divorce and my determination to stay in my school district resulted in me crashing on couches, living in spare bedrooms and basements, and at one point, sharing an apartment with my sister. From my freshman year in high school to my graduation, my teacher Melanie Shelnutt provided the stability I needed in my life. As a result, I now lead teams with the same power of positive influence she instilled in her students.

It wasn't until I became an executive working for global organizations that I realized the importance of Ms. Shelnutt's impact on my life during those four years—specifically, how it would shape the type of leader I would become and how I would apply that kind of influence in developing global teams.

Her influence taught me to be positive in all situations, accept others (because you never know what they might be experiencing), and always keep moving forward. Some of the concepts she instilled in me that I embody today are:

- **Dream big.** I was a ward of the court, and many believed I wouldn't graduate from high school. The odds were against me, but I was determined to get a college degree and prove them wrong. To this day, I encourage those who work with me to always dream bigger and never stop reaching for the stars.

- **Find your purpose.** The struggles I faced as a young adult have led me to empower the next generation of leaders to never quit, regardless of how hard things seem at the time. I regularly speak to crowds of graduates, interns, and young people in schools to share my story so that I might reach that one student who is thinking about giving up. I didn't, and I want them to know that determination and hard work pay off.

- **Ignore the cynics.** There will always be those who doubt your ability, challenge you, and try to derail your goals. Ignore them! I would rather be admired by the 1 percent who support me than falsely "loved" by the 99 percent who criticize me.

- **Regardless of role, respect those around you.** Treat everyone you meet equally—from custodian to principal, CEO to mailroom clerk, intern to executive. Each of us plays an important part in everyday life, and being a leader means respecting every role equally.

- **Be authentic.** Always remember that the perception of your intelligence, your influence of others, and your ability to lead others come from within you. So be true to yourself. I believe in transparency. When you meet me, you get who I am—no fluff—and I challenge my teams to be the same.

In four short years, Ms. Shelnutt taught me to embrace my journey, stand up for myself, and fight for what I wanted. She believed in me and taught me how to believe in myself.

The influence of her forty-year tenure in teaching (1979-2019) has impacted a conservative estimate of more than 10,000 students, including thirty-five homerooms, multiple cheerleading squads, and the various clubs she led.

Even during some of the most difficult times in her own life, Ms. Shelnutt exuded nothing but positive radiance, and it was shared by those around her.

Her energy was—and is—contagious!

So, Ms. Shelnutt, as you enter into your retirement in 2019, know that there are thousands of us giving you a standing ovation, and because of you, we will always remember to Rock On and Spread The Love—ROASTL!

Heather Monahan

Having reached the C-suite in media with more than twenty years of successful leadership experience, Heather Monahan is a women's empowerment expert and founder of Boss In Heels. She is a social media influencer, keynote speaker, Glass Ceiling award recipient, bestselling author of Confidence Creator, *and brand ambassador for Perry Ellis International's women's clothing brand, Rafaella. She is committed to advancing others via her website www.heathermonahan.com.*

....

Early in my life, I thought I needed to do everything myself in order to prove my worth. Over the years, I have learned that no one succeeds in this world alone. In fact, I learned that the strongest and most confident people ask for help and lean on others when they need support. One example that sticks out for me is the time a good friend came to my defense when I needed help.

Rafe D'Amico had worked for me for a few years and over that time had become a personal friend as well. Often we would travel on business trips together, and we really enjoyed the camaraderie of closing deals and accomplishing our goals together on the various trips. A few years back, I was given the opportunity to take the main stage at a large National Association of Broadcasters event, and naturally Rafe and many other people from work were in attendance. The event was held at a massive hotel in Austin, where we were all staying. When the award that I was giving away was met with boos because the company that won was not in attendance, I decided to do a little dance and make a joke in order to quash an ugly moment at the event. The crowd found my bit funny, and everyone started laughing and clapping.

As I walked off the stage, people began running up to tell me what a great job I had done and how I had turned a potentially bad situation into a positive one. I felt like I was walking on air. I was proud of myself and couldn't wait to high-five my coworkers and bask in the limelight. Something I didn't know back then is that when you put yourself out there, you are not only going to get praise, but you will inevitably get your haters' attention, too.

Rafe, some of our other coworkers, and I were all smiles as we headed to the bar to toast my mini victory. Random people were approaching to congratulate me on my save, and I was feeling very full of myself. I excused myself from the group to go to the ladies' room. As I turned down the hall, a man grabbed my arm very tight and I couldn't pull free. He started verbally attacking me and telling me what a joke I was. He was so angry. I had never met this man before and had no idea why he was attacking me, but I was scared and alone. I finally broke free and ran into the ladies' room, where I started crying.

When I was able to pull myself together, I headed back over to Rafe and the group from work. Rafe could see that I had been crying, and I told him and the others what had happened. I also said I would never get back on stage again because it just wasn't worth it. That is when Rafe leaped up and took off. He chased down that man from the bathroom and had a very serious exchange with him.

A few minutes later, Rafe and the crazy man approached me together. Rafe had confronted the man and demanded that he apologize to me because he wanted me to get back on stage again, and he needed me to know that this was about the crazy person and not about me. It turns out that this man was not crazy. He was depressed because he had just been fired from his job. He hated seeing others who looked like they were succeeding because it reminded him that he was not successful. He told me he was wrong, he was sorry, and I had done a great job.

In that brief encounter, Rafe taught me two very important things: When the people around you support you and stand up for you, it makes you feel very special and loved. And when you shine your light, haters will come, but it is always about them and not about you.

Because Rafe stood up for me and taught me these lessons, I have taken countless stages since that incident and have faced my share of haters with a smile. I often call Rafe and share my most recent hater moments with him so we can laugh about that infamous night. I now realize that strong people ask for help and lean on those who support them. I want to give a standing O to Rafe for always standing by me, chasing down my haters, and having my back. No one in this world succeeds alone.

Talia Mota

Talia Mota has dedicated her life as a scientist to discovering a cure for HIV. She has volunteered all over the world, fostering her passion and working with people living with HIV and AIDS in Cambodia, Nicaragua, India, and Botswana. She completed her Ph.D. in Australia and after ten years abroad has finally returned to the United States, where she continues her research. Her focus is on purging the latent HIV reservoir by harnessing the power of the immune system to kill cells infected with HIV.

....

If you want to find that one thing that excites you every day, fills you with passion, and challenges you at the same time, go looking for it.

Quitting my job in San Francisco and moving to Cambodia was not easy, but it led me to a series of unforgettable adventures that made it easy for me to dedicate my life to finding a cure for HIV. And that led me to Kopano Boineelo Mmalane—or KP, as everyone calls her—the woman to whom I want to give a huge standing ovation.

I first met her in an elevator in Durban, South Africa, at the International AIDS Conference in 2016. I was studying for my Ph.D. in Australia and researching a cure for HIV, and she was an HIV/AIDS doctor in Botswana who was about to start a rural placement. I'll never forget the look on her face when I told her I'd come visit her in Botswana one day. "Sure you will." Less than a year later, I submitted my Ph.D., bought a one-way ticket to Namibia, went camping in the World Heritage Site sand dunes of the Namib Desert, then hitchhiked to KP's village in Ghanzi, Botswana, where the apparent danger was being hunted by lions.

KP was a general practitioner—and so much more. I'd never met a GP who ran a malnutrition clinic for starving children at the same time she was dealing with botched home abortions that were otherwise illegal and required to give a clean bill of health to approve public lashings for individuals who were punished for being homosexual.

After I cuddled children all morning who were brought back to life because of KP's efforts, her next patient was handed to me—a one-month-old wrapped tightly in a blanket. As we unraveled the blanket, I was blown away by how stunning her tiny features were, her tiny nose, her perfect eyelashes, and how peaceful she looked. As we continued to unwrap the blanket, I saw the lesions down her body and areas where bones and ligaments were sticking out through her skin. And even if I knew it, I couldn't accept it. I was holding a baby who had died from AIDS. I was holding a dead baby.

I cried in a corner for most of the afternoon, but KP demonstrated a bravery I had never seen before. She was calm and compassionate, but she was also used to seeing this day in and day out. Once the sun was long gone, she came back for me. "I'm not letting you leave here with that as your last experience. Come."

I followed her into the night to an OR where a tribal woman needed an emergency C-section or she and her unborn child would die. KP, not a surgeon, was about to perform a huge surgery. I watched as she sliced through skin, ripped through muscle, and extracted a being from within the womb. The baby was under stress and needed oxygen. I couldn't breathe until it breathed. I had never seen a baby being born. They handed me the baby, wrapped in a blanket. Again, tears rolled down my cheeks. But this time, they were tears of happiness.

My day started with death and ended with life. The admiration I have for KP is unparalleled—and my own passion to cure HIV was reignited. As I move back to the USA after ten years abroad, ready to continue researching a cure during my postdoctoral fellowship, I look forward to fifteen-hour days in the lab; this is *my* day in and day out, my contribution. I will not stop until HIV is gone, or until I am dead.

When I think of KP, I see an extraordinary woman my age who has been in the trenches of HIV and AIDS, sees and lives through the death and devastation every single day, and yet continues to fight. She reminds me how to find strength and reminds me to simply be happy—that all we need to lead our lives are love and passion and to remember our WHY.

Find what excites you, fills you with passion, and challenges you at the same time—and chase it to the end of the world. Just when I couldn't be more inspired by a single human being, she told me she's been accepted into a cardiothoracic surgery program in South Africa and will become Botswana's first heart surgeon—and this was her dream.

Mark Moyer

Mark Moyer is a career coach and business growth strategist with more than twenty years' experience guiding athletes and entrepreneurs to their full potential. He wrote Win Again, *a job search playbook not just for the athletes for whom it was originally designed but anyone seeking to excel. He is a speaker and* Forbes *contributor and is widely quoted in business and sports-related publications. Moyer graduated from Colgate University with a degree in economics.*

....

You've heard it before from a variety of sources and in all kinds of variations: Treat others as you would like to be treated. I'd like to take it a step further: I try my best to treat others even better than I might expect or hope to be treated in return.

My mother passed away a few years ago after a nearly twenty-year battle with Alzheimer's, and for those of you who have had a family member, friend, or acquaintance go through it, typically it is the caregivers who suffer the most because they see the steady and precipitous decline in their loved one's mental state.

However, this is not about my mother's fight with the disease but more so a standing ovation for what she taught me during my very early and formative years.

I have countless memories of seeing my mother make others laugh, whether it was at the clothing store she dragged me to when it was time to buy me a new pair of wallabees, corduroy pants, or wide-collared shirts. Yes, it was the 1970s, and I was often mortified when my mother would walk into Caldor department store and announce to everyone within earshot that she was there to outfit me in some new digs. Although I tended to be a bit embarrassed by her behavior, I noticed that the salespeople always smiled and replied back in kind.

My mother would make waiters, gas station attendants, grocery store workers, and anyone else she encountered not only smile and laugh but certainly remember her the next time she entered their lives.

I have tried to emulate that behavior throughout my life. I do my best to share with anyone I encounter that same smile and laugh, with the understanding that I respect the job they do or the service they provide, regardless of how others might treat them.

Perhaps more important, if I am having a challenging day or maybe just had a call or meeting that delivered a negative result, I do my best to push it aside for my next encounter or conversation because I always want people to see me in a positive light. After all, it is so much easier to get the desired result from someone if they see you in that positive light. If you greet someone with a smile, it is difficult for them not to smile back.

I have spent virtually my entire career giving people advice. Whether it is about finding a job, starting a new business, improving sales strategies, or doing all kinds of things in between, I always advise my clients to treat everyone equally and tell them that almost anyone can be the one person who makes a connection that results in great success. I have personally found that virtually everyone I make contact with can provide me with value, and I try my best to treat them that way. And this is the message I pass on to others.

I have lived most of my adult life in New York City, a place that can take its toll on the human spirit if you let it. Yet I have found that it is also the perfect place to smile and laugh, elevate those around me, and push forward with the values and traits that my mother taught me so well all those years ago. Follow her lead: Make others smile and treat everyone with the same level of respect, and you will see it reflected back to you in even greater form.

Steve Nudelberg

Steve Nudelberg is an author, sales trainer, consultant, keynote speaker, and serial salesman and entrepreneur. He created On the Ball, a company that invests time and talent in emerging businesses and corporate teams to help them grow. His 27 core leadership rules of engagement are laid out in his book Confessions of a Serial Salesman. *He founded his own sales and marketing company that offers sales strategy, messaging, brand identity, sales and leadership training, and Arrangemenship™ (business development) as well as other services.*

....

By most people's standards, I am a confident guy. It's always been that way, or at least that's what I was taught.

I was born into a family of successful salespeople, starting with my Grandfather Sid, the best of the best. And then the skill was passed down to my dad, Stan, then to my cousin Andrew, then me, and now to my boys. Although my boys are not in the direct-sales game, they are proof that we are always selling.

I was taught at a very young age that you are always selling one thing—yourself—and that lesson lives within me today. Learning about the importance of a work ethic, creating my own style and presence, building relationships, and learning how to communicate were invaluable.

I had a typical middle-class upbringing in a Long Island suburb called Baldwin, then moved to South Florida to finish high school and then off to college.

Starting at a young age, I would accompany my dad to work on Saturdays. My dad and grandfather were in the retail ladies' shoe business and had a few very successful stores.

On those learning Saturdays, I played stock boy to the twenty-plus sales guys who manned the sales floor. The stores were high-fashion, so the guys were decked out from head to toe—polished nails, polished shoes, sparkling cufflinks, outstanding ties. You get the picture, right? Straight off the cover of GQ.

Each Saturday, I would get the chance to watch first-hand the artistry that once existed in the sales world. These guys were magicians in creating instant bonds with their prospects, finding out all the key points to secure trust, and then effortlessly moving to the close, with shoes, bags, and accessories included.

Talk about an education! I was overwhelmed, and it was all orchestrated by the band leader, my Grandfather Sid, with my dad at his wing.

I can still remember those years of wanting to be just like them.

Those early days of watching were valuable in so many ways and ultimately turned into an opportunity to be one of those very guys on the sales floor.

Once I was one of them, the heat got turned up.

Although we were a family business, there was no nepotism. In fact, I believe they were harder on me than all the others and with good reason. I can still remember my grandfather really working me hard, so much so that I was ready to go after him.

I would go to my dad to complain, and although he would offer sympathy, he told me we all have to pay our dues if we want to get to the top.

Then I would confront my grandfather, and with his undeniable charm and style, he would offer this gem: "Every time I break you down, you will get up and be stronger, and that's how you win the game."

Those are days I will always treasure because they made me who I am. So the takeaway is this: Success leaves clues.

There are undeniable truths about successful people. They all have great passion for what they do. They are undyingly willing to sacrifice, have an unbelievable work ethic, and will ultimately play three roles in their lives: students, teachers, and motivators.

I am giving my Grandfather Sid a standing O for showing me how it's done. You have left an incredible legacy that I strive to live up to every day.

Here are the words I used in his farewell service in 1993: "You have lived, loved, and danced better than most. Now in your new home, show those 'bastards' how to party."

Colin O'Brady

As one of the world's elite endurance athletes, Colin O'Brady has accomplished incredible feats: racing in a triathlon professionally for the United States, summiting Mount Everest, and holding two of the most prestigious mountaineering world records. He did it all after overcoming a devastating accident to prove that anything is possible. He is a graduate of Yale University and a highly sought-after public speaker with a reputation that inspires.

....

Nine years ago, I woke up in a hospital bed in Thailand with both of my legs bandaged from my toes to my hips. I had been severely burned in a fire, and the doctors warned me that I might never walk again normally. Looking back, I am not sure which was worse: the physical pain searing through my body or the deep emotional darkness that threatened to overwhelm me. I was twenty-two years old at the time, recently graduated from college and getting ready to embark on life as a young professional. As a collegiate swimmer and lifelong athlete, I had taken for granted my ability to live an active life, and in an instant, my entire future seemed to be at risk. Would I ever be the same?

After several days of broken phone calls and trans-Pacific travel, my mother arrived on the remote Thai island of Koh Samui to find me incapacitated in my hospital bed. I had just come out of another surgery, and there was a cat running around my bed in the ICU. Needless to say, this was not the place either of us wanted to be under any circumstance.

I know now that for my mother this was one of the hardest moments to face: your child helplessly injured and in pain. To my mom's credit, she didn't show any weakness in the face of this tragedy; rather, she instilled confidence and strength. While I was slipping into the negative delirium of an uncertain future, she was the rock by my bedside. And with one simple phrase, she changed my life forever. She said, "Let's set a goal."

Mom, I want to give you a standing O!

I have always been a very goal-driven person, but in this moment, any goal or forward motion seemed impossible. However, after a number of long conversations, we came up with the idea that I would one day complete a triathlon. This goal seemed audacious to say the least, given my diagnosis and the fact that I hadn't taken a single step in over a month. But the goal was fixed in my mind. I knew from that point onward I would work toward that goal to prove to myself that I could not only walk again normally, but also run and thrive.

With the large goal of completing my first triathlon looming, I was still faced with the reality of legs so injured I couldn't walk. The big goal was ever present in my mind; however, the key to achieving any lofty goal is the daily execution of incremental goals to get there. For me, this was literally taking one step at a time.

Finally, I arrived back in the United States, but I was still wheelchair-bound. My first incremental goal was to find a way to move out of my wheelchair. My mom placed a chair from our kitchen table in front of my wheelchair and said, "Colin, your goal today is to take your first step. Get up from your wheelchair and move to this chair in front of you." It took a couple days to master this "first step." With each progressive day, the second chair was placed a few steps farther away. One step became five and then ten. I remember celebrating the day I could walk from the living room couch to the dining room table. Progress was slow, but each one of these incremental steps was crucial to achieving my bigger goal of completing a triathlon. My mom never stopped pushing me and believing in me.

It was a year of hard work, rehab, and recovery until I began to feel like myself again. Still my resolve to complete a triathlon was fixed in my mind. I signed up for the Chicago Triathlon and gave myself another six months to train. Just over eighteen months after my burn accident, I completed the Chicago Olympic-distance triathlon (one-mile swim, twenty-five-mile bike ride, 6.2-mile run). Little did I know a huge surprise was in store for me that day. When the results were announced hours after I had crossed the finish line, I learned that not only had I completed my goal of finishing the race, but I had won the entire race, coming in first over 4,000 other competitors.

It was an unforgettable moment and proof that even when the odds are stacked against us, we are capable of achieving amazing things when we set our minds to it. Without my mother's guidance during this tragedy, my fate would have been dramatically different.

At that time, I had recently begun what I thought would be a lifelong career in the financial industry working as a commodities trader. However, my Chicago Triathlon victory opened the door to a professional athletic career. Although this was a far less lucrative and certain path, I was inspired to take this leap of faith and continue to follow my dreams. With many years of hindsight, I can safely say I have no regrets. I have gone on to represent the USA in professional triathlon competition in twenty-five countries on six continents. It has been a dream come true to say the least. I have had many successes as well as failures on the racecourse, but no matter the outcome, each time I cross the finish line, I'm deeply grateful and proud remembering the goal I set while laying in a Thai hospital bed. That goal got me through when it looked like I might never be able to walk normally, let alone run, again.

Two years ago, after finishing another successful triathlon season, a new goal began to percolate in my mind. My excitement for pushing my body and being a professional athlete had not waned, and I felt the urge to use that platform to do something greater than simply win on the racecourse. It was then that I realized my good fortune. I grew up with many amazing role models and supporters who helped me succeed when the chips were stacked against me. I began to brainstorm ways in which I could reach a larger audience and share the lessons I had learned about overcoming obstacles and the power of the human spirit. From that brainstorm with my fiancée, Jenna, my next goal was born.

We coined our project BEYOND 7/2. The aim was to break the world record for completing the Explorers Grand Slam, a mountaineering challenge to climb the tallest mountain on each of the seven continents

(Everest, Denali, Kilimanjaro, etc.) and complete expeditions across the last degree of latitude to reach the North and South Poles. Fewer than fifty people had ever completed this challenge and only two in under a calendar year. I was aiming to become the fastest to complete the feat in under five months.

The greater purpose behind the project was to share the story in real time to a large audience of students around the world to hopefully inspire them to dream big and realize the value of living active, healthy lives.

This challenge became my new "big goal," but it was going to take hundreds of incremental goals and steps to become a world record holder. Without the unyielding support of Jenna, I would never have been able to accomplish all these steps. She put other career opportunities on hold to work full-time (and unpaid) to help build our vision.

We had an idea, but putting it into action is the hard part. We needed to raise money from corporate sponsors to complete the expeditions. We formed a nonprofit organization to benefit our charitable work with the kids. We had to figure out a media strategy to tell this story and drive impact. We needed to figure out how to plan, organize, and execute on nine back-to-back expeditions in the most remote parts of the world. Not to mention that I needed to train to make sure my body was ready physically. Our hands were full to say the least.

There were many times when it looked like I would never get the chance to begin my journey because the funding and logistics were proving to be a huge hurdle to clear. Even in the face of significant odds stacked against us, we stayed focused each day on the incremental goals and hoped that our hard work would eventually pay off.

On January 4, 2016, I began my expedition to the South Pole, the first expedition in the BEYOND 7/2 world record attempt. I battled minus-40-degree temperatures while dragging a hundred-pound sled with all my supplies. It was incredibly difficult. When times got tough out there, I drew strength from my past and knowing that if I kept putting one foot in front of the other, I would eventually reach my goal.

Along the journey, some of the biggest challenges came when I faced setbacks that were out of my control. I often thought that if I failed to break the world record because I lacked the strength, it would be difficult to process, but as long as I gave it everything I had, then I could hold my head high and be proud despite the failure. However, if the world record was derailed by something out of my control—such as a cancelled flight, bad weather, or an avalanche—it would be a tough pill to swallow. As the journey progressed, I learned the power of being flexible in the face of adversity. In all our lives, many things are out of our control. All we can do is prepare as best as we can and be flexible when Plan A doesn't work out.

No one summited Mount Everest in 2015 due to a natural disaster. Many people doubted my ability to climb Everest in 2016 because of this—not to mention complete eight other expeditions in succession. I chose to focus on the positive and ask myself, "Why not me?" By keeping a positive headspace and believing I could achieve this goal, I remained determined to beat the odds. And when my own positive self-talk failed me, Jenna was right there to encourage me to keep fighting.

At 26,000 feet on Mount Everest as I attempted the summit, I was caught in a major windstorm. I knew my summit attempt was over and that I would need to descend the mountain without reaching the summit. Again, many people questioned the likelihood of success on Everest, saying the expedition was surely over because it would be too hard to summon the energy and courage to try a second time. Four days later, I found triumph when I reached the summit of Mount Everest and completed the eighth expedition of the Explorers Grand Slam world record.

The path to the top isn't always a straight line. I climbed back down the mountain before making my way to the summit, but even as I was retreating after my first attempt, I believed I could somehow find a way. There are bound to be setbacks on any path, and even when it feels like you are walking in the wrong direction or headed backward, never give up!

On the summit of Denali eight days later, I completed the BEYOND 7/2 challenge and in the process broke two world records, fulfilling Jenna and my dreams. This journey was never just about me and my personal achievements. Just as I hoped to share this story with kids around the world to inspire them to dream big and strive for success, I hope that anyone reading this realizes the power of goal setting and the resilience of the human spirit. I am no different from anyone else. I had two choices when I was in that hospital bed in Thailand: accept the diagnosis or dig deep and fight against the odds. I am living proof that no matter what setbacks you face in life and no matter your circumstances, if you believe in yourself and refuse to quit, anything is possible.

None of this would have been possible without the unconditional love and belief that my mom and Jenna have had for me. They have taught me the values of never giving up even in my darkest hours. They are my heroes. I honor them with a standing O!

Alex Ortiz

Alex Ortiz is a technology evangelist in the blockchain industry. His background in neuroscience, education, software sales, and blockchain has given him an appreciation for how people, knowledge, science, and technology can be used to solve the important challenges of our time. He is an avid optimist, and his life's mission is to use our best ideas in the service of our best ideals.

....

There is nothing in the world more beautiful than a friendship. For twenty years, I've been reminded of that lesson by my lifelong friend Winston.

We met in our second year of high school, and we didn't like each other all that much at first. Like two sides of a coin, we initially couldn't see to the other side to know that we were more alike than we realized. But as the flips mounted and as heads and tails were shown over time to be distinct yet not so different, Winston and I grew close. Conversations, musical tastes, philosophical concerns, moral values, inside jokes, cultural references, shared hardships, and the thousand other points of experience that make up the constellation of a true friendship gradually yielded the realization that we would remain friends for life.

Through Winston, I've learned to be patient with myself, forgive others, and elevate the needs of loved ones above my own. I've learned wisdom, nuance, and the importance of recognizing your own strengths and operating with a light touch when dealing with other people. I've learned to retain perspective during storms, remember years-ago promises I've made to myself, and navigate difficult feelings and difficult chapters with a growth mindset and the confidence that's earned through years of resilience.

But perhaps my favorite lesson, one that I learned years ago from my dear friend, is that relationships of nearly any kind revolve around two things: understanding the other person's fears and seeing that person clearly. At the time, I was having trouble connecting with someone I cared for deeply. Naturally, I reached out to Winston for advice. Like any good friend, he listened to my situation impartially and with a generous ear. After I finished talking, he patiently and helpfully relayed the timeless pearl of wisdom popularized by Stephen Covey: People should always seek to understand before seeking to be understood.

You see, every person wants to feel heard and be seen. Operating with kindness and patience toward someone's fears and acting and responding to who they are, not who we wish them to be, is a difficult but worthy, lifelong project.

In this life lesson, there is also an important leadership lesson. Many of the problems we face in society—in our relationships, at our workplaces, in our nations, and throughout the world—originate in some way from not applying this teaching. Consider everything required to do so: selflessness, listening, empathy, compassion. Exploring someone else's universe as closely as you would your own. Defaulting to learning who a person is and what they care about in order to offer better companionship. Leading from the other person's feelings and location. Starting fundamentally from a place of concern.

All of them require ongoing work to put effectively into practice, but they result in stronger connections with others, healthier outcomes for ourselves, and a foundation from which to grow closer as people, not drift apart. They also act as bulwarks against relationship-destroyers, such as arrogance or contempt, and daylight some of the blind spots that contribute to foolish decisions. And as with all wisdom, applying to ourselves what we know is good for others creates a richness that we can then spend more freely with the rest of the world.

I now realize that my friend long ago extended to me the very thing he hoped I would learn to extend to others: the opportunity to have another person understand your fears, see you clearly, and share with you from a place of deep empathy and selfless compassion. A lesson as beautiful as this is itself a gift.

Here's to the lifelong friend I've been so honored to learn from—a hug and a standing O to you, Winston.

Robert Hamilton Owens

Robert Hamilton Owens is a: mountain climber, radio and TV personality, keynote speaker, minister, Ironman, philanthropist, triathlete, Special Ops Pararescueman, and father of five. But there's one title that best describes him: the fittest sixty-six-year-old in the world. Raised as a special-needs child who was unable to play kickball with his classmates due to the corrective shoes he wore through sixth grade, in 1973, he entered the U.S. Air Force Special Operations School to train as a Pararescueman, the Air Force equivalent of a Navy SEAL. He was one of only 157 men who graduated.

....

I was too small for football in junior high. Tried baseball and basketball, but they just didn't seem to be a fit. Other kids were bigger, faster, stronger, and more athletic.

I am adopted. My adoptive father was a Stanford grad and an academic. He wasn't into sports. But my mom was a physical education major out of UCLA. She encouraged me to find something I liked and could be good at.

She took me to a swim school when I was three years old. I loved it. By junior high school, I was surfing a lot, and anything that had to do with the water seemed to come easily for me.

I had a tough time in school from the sixth grade on because my mom was sick with lupus. Bad grades followed. But a few male teachers started to encourage me and believe in me.

The big turning point was when I was encouraged to join our high school swim team and water polo team. Our coach was Jon Urbanchek, who was a Hungarian Olympic water polo player and swimmer. He had been in the U.S. for three years and didn't speak much English. But he found a way to communicate.

When he saw me, he was kind to me but didn't think much of me. All the good swimmers came from younger group swimming programs. Some had been swimming for six or seven years already. Here I was starting in ninth grade.

But I remember him saying in his barely understandable English, "If you work hard, you can be a good water polo player and maybe get us a point in swimming." In swim meets, first place got five points, second place received three points, and there was one point for third place. I wanted to get a point.

It was just enough confidence in me to encourage me that maybe I could do well and make a difference if I worked hard.

So for the next three years, I learned to work hard. Just so you understand "work hard": Jon was an Olympian. He ultimately left Anaheim High School after developing our program into a nationally ranked high school program that produced many All-Americans to take a job coaching swimming and water polo at Long Beach State in Long Beach, California. From there, he became the head swim coach at the University of Michigan and the U.S. Olympic swim coach. He is the swimming grandfather to Michael Phelps and others. He is in the International Swimming Hall of Fame.

So when I say we worked hard, we worked until we were exhausted daily. Up to three workouts a day and 6,000 yards a day at times. But we loved to win. And we won a lot.

I wasn't an All-American swimmer, but I learned to work hard and loved it. Still, I was average.

I graduated from high school at 5'11" and about 155 pounds.

In time, I enrolled at Orange Coast College, where I rowed crew. Again, the program was outstanding and was nationally known for its competitiveness for a two-year college.

We worked hard. We were on the water by 6:30 a.m. after arriving for PT at 5:45 a.m. I have never done anything as hard as crew.

I learned to drive myself to the point of throwing up and nearly passing out. But I was average. There were much better oarsmen than myself, but I loved to work hard. It was my only hope of being on the team.

Then came Pararescue and the Air Force. During high school, many of the water polo players were beach lifeguards. The tryouts were hard, especially since the college water polo players and swimmers tried out, too. We would have seventy to ninety guys try out for five to ten positions.

I wasn't as fast as many of them, but I outsmarted them. I took two firsts and a third out of three events as a sophomore in high school. I was an ocean guy, and they were mainly pool guys. I knew I was average. But I could work harder and be more strategic than most.

Many of the lifeguards were being recruited to be Navy SEALs. They were looking for water guys who could go all day.

But the Air Force was recruiting lifeguards to be Special Ops Combat Paramedics. If you liked rescuing people, this was the next step up into the big leagues.

At twenty-three, I went into the Air Force to be a Pararescueman. I was still an average, general type. But I wasn't average to those trying out. Over one-hundred guys tried out in basic training Saturday tryouts. The PJ Indoc program took about thirty of us. And out of those thirty who went through two years of Pararescue training, about fifteen made it. I made it and was made team leader. I discovered I wasn't average anymore. I knew how to outwork others.

When I got out of the Air Force, I read the famous Sports Illustrated article in 1979 about a crazy, mind-boggling endurance event in Honolulu called a triathlon. When it moved to Kona in its fourth year, it became the Ironman Triathlon.

I knew I had to attempt it, but those were long distances back then. So I went to work to work hard at swimming, biking, and running. I worked out really hard because I was afraid. I had no idea if I could do it. But I spent six months, five to six times a week, pressing myself beyond what anyone thought I should do.

As it turned out, I made it with those famous one-hundred people who showed up in January 1980. I finished thirty-ninth after passing out in a guy's driveway just past the halfway point in the marathon. I was in the group of sixteen to twenty place guys when I blew up from dehydration. My pee was dark brown. But with some help and fluids, I got up in fifty-first place and raced back to thirty-ninth place.

I had learned how to go past limits from hard training.

I have finished twelve Ironman competitions now and still enjoy the challenge of not riding the bike once before an Ironman and only swimming a month before the event. Why? Because I like to stay in good enough shape to challenge myself to just do it.

I am an average guy who has learned to do what others don't think is average.

I was tired of being reminded or told I was old. At sixty-three, I heard about two super-challenging events:

1. The World Marathon Challenge, consisting of seven marathons in seven days on seven continents.

2. SEALFIT's Kokoro fifty-hour challenge, modeled on the Navy SEALs' Hell Week. For me, it would be like going back to Pararescue training but at sixty-three. Kokoro is a mix of CrossFit Games strength and endurance testing and the Navy SEALs' Hell Week—however, it goes for fifty straight hours. It is the toughest event in America for many reasons.

I knew I was not strong enough to do either. And the Kokoro guys told many people that they crushed the Ironman guys who showed up. All the Ironmen who had previously attempted it had quit the first time they tried it. So I knew I had to do it. And best of all, I'd be the oldest person to ever attempt it. I wanted that record.

I believed it would take me at least a year to get strong enough to pass the entrance test. I could do three dead-hang pull-ups, and I had to do fifteen. Plus, I had to do one-hundred pull-ups in an event within Kokoro.

I joined a local CrossFit gym and began training to get strong and gain endurance. I was at either the 5:30 a.m. class or the 8 a.m. class five days a week. After six months of my CrossFit training, I went down to SEALFIT on a Saturday morning to test myself against SEALFIT-trained athletes. I barely survived one of their one-hour workouts. But then I saw other forty-five-year-old to sixty-year-old men repeat the same workout the next hour. They were beasts!

After a year, I was able to finish those Saturday morning workouts at SEALFIT. But then I blew up my right shoulder doing box jumps and had to have surgery. I couldn't do a push-up for six months and watched my body lose all its gains.

But finally my right shoulder began to come around, and I started all over again in January 2017.

In February, the SEALFIT guys told me about an event in Greece in May. The 300 of Sparta endurance march was 238 miles in eight days, or about thirty miles a day. It was a fundraiser to support a foundation named for a Navy SEAL killed in the 2012 terrorist attack on the U.S. consulate in Benghazi, Libya, and to support the Navy SEALs Foundation.

I figured it would be a good testing event for the World Marathon Challenge, so I signed up.

It was tough. The heat ate our feet. It was the most miserable experience of my life as my feet blistered badly and swelled up on Day One. The rest of the week just got worse. But I made it, as did most of the others. Wonderfully, it reminded me that I could tolerate more pain than I ever thought I could.

In June, I heard about an event in August that was a twenty-six-mile marathon of run-swim-run-swim. I figured I was in shape, so on a Sunday morning, I and a bunch of young guys started from the San Clemente Pier and went twenty-six miles in nine hours to the Balboa Pier in Newport Beach, California. I was the oldest participant by twenty-five years.

It was tough because whenever you were not swimming, you had to be running and not walking. And the waves were booming that day. We all made it, but I should never try to keep up with eighteen-year-old to twenty-five-year-old lifeguard athletes again. It was fun, sort of.

In October 2017, I showed up for Kokoro. The instructors asked me why I was there, and I told them I wanted the record of being the oldest finisher ever. Plus, I would be the first Pararescueman to do it. The Navy guys loved it. They relished the opportunity to see if they could get me to quit.

Somehow, I survived. It was brutal. If I'd known how hard it would be, I would never have attempted it. At the end, a number of Navy SEAL instructors congratulated me. A couple said they knew I'd never quit because I was a PJ or Pararescueman. We never do.

In November, since I was in shape, I knocked out my twelfth Ironman. I didn't train at all for it, except a little swimming. It was the easiest thing I had done.

Finally, the World Marathon Challenge came in late January. After the Ironman, I stopped everything but running. All the muscle I had developed from CrossFit fell off. I lost ten pounds. I knew I had to be mentally used to deep fatigue so I began to do twenty-mile runs with a twenty-pound weight vest. The goal was to train harder than I imagined the event would be. Or outwork anybody else.

It was a wild thing, but I knocked out the 777. It was really challenging because we had four night marathons, which I wasn't expecting. Plus, the first marathon in Antarctica and the second one in Cape Town, South Africa, had to be done in less than twenty-four hours. The Antarctic marathon ended in subzero weather. The next day in Cape Town, it was

90 degrees. It was wild.

As a non-runner, those seven marathons taught me how to handle being miserable. Once I figured it out, it was just a mental game. Mental toughness is a learned skill.

So five major endurance events in eight months proved that seniors can still stay in the game with the younger guys. We just need to train harder than the event. It is fun to do the unbelievable. It reminds me what it feels like to live.

Diana Picasso

Diana Picasso is an art historian, curator, and co-founder of an investment 24K gold jewelry company called Mené.

• •

It was my fortuitous ancestry—at least in part—that exposed me at an early age to the things of art. By things, I mean beauty, exaltation, excitement, anguish. Everything that makes us living.

My grandfather, the illustrious artist Pablo Picasso, was well aware that one could aspire to a thousand discoveries. I discovered this research-driven emulation myself as a student of art history at Sorbonne University in the city of Paris, where I grew up. At the time, I was fascinated by Professor Antoine Schnapper, who taught the history of seventeenth-century French art and was particularly interested in the history of collections and the art market—in short, the relationship between human beings and objects.

He was fascinated by both the psychological and sociological aspects, and I found them equally fascinating. I understood that beyond the work of art itself, there was the person who knew how to appreciate it and the person who knew how to breathe life into it. And then there was the dogged collector who gave meaning to his life through an illusory accumulation.

This very rapport with materiality (or lack of materiality) is what naturally led me to special people who were a source of inspiration. Among them is my dear friend Klaus Biesenbach, director of MoMA PS1, who one day introduced me to Alejandro Jodorowsky and his wife, Pascale. Alejandro became my mentor. This exquisite human being is the Chilean filmmaker who made the legendary El Topo, The Holy Mountain, and recently The Dance of Reality. Magician of the soul, Alejandro loves to transform works of art and performance into acts of psychomagic. He does art to heal, for otherwise art is of no interest to him and is reduced to an affirmation of individuality. However, for art to have therapeutic virtues, the contact between therapeutic practice and artistic practice has to result in an encounter.

Mexico is where he developed the concept of psychomagic, a form of therapy that proposes to treat all sorts of pains using symbolic acts directly connected with the subconscious. For example, Alejandro once told me about someone extremely shy who came to see him. Since this person was uncomfortable with his body, Alejandro told him to go out and walk around naked. And to make sure he didn't get stopped for exhibitionism, Alejandro advised him to have a friend film him so they could say it was an artistic performance if need be.

Psychomagic aims to avoid repeating the problems inherited from our ancestors. Consequently, Alejandro strives to break the vicious circles in which we are caught intellectually, emotionally, sexual-creatively, or materially. For my part, this wise, brilliant friend succeeded through an initial tarot reading to bring another dimension to my passion for art and more reasons to share it with others who are not as privileged as I am. Art shows can indeed be empowered to bring light, beauty, and richness and to heal wounds.

Preston Pysh

Preston Pysh is the founder of Pylon Holding Company, an ethics-based leader, entrepreneur, and international bestselling author. He is also the co-host and founder of The Investor's Podcast *and an investment contributor to* Forbes *and* Yahoo Finance. *Pysh has over a decade of operations management and project management experience for programs in excess of $1 billion dollars. Specialties include aerospace engineering, military acquisition, security analysis, economics, publishing, online business, and SEO.*

I once had the opportunity to interview a genius. The man's name was Ed Thorp. Although Ed was eighty-four years old when I talked to him, you would have thought he was at least twenty years younger.

Ed became famous for writing a book on how to count cards when playing blackjack. After that, he started an investment firm and achieved 19.1 percent annual returns for the nineteen years the firm was in business. More impressively, out of the 230 months Ed was trading in the markets, he had 227 months of positive returns. Not only did he trade over $100 billion with his firm, but he also created the first wearable computer that allowed him to statistically beat the odds of roulette by applying Newtonian physics to calculate where the ball might land. To say he was brilliant was clearly an understatement.

The thing I remember most about my discussion with Ed was his self-awareness. During the interview, I asked him an economics question that I felt was reasonably straightforward. The question itself wasn't important, but the way he responded was. I asked Ed, "Do you think central banks are going to cause the next stock market crash by keeping interest rates too low for too long?"

Most people would have pontificated about different ideas that beat around the question. But Ed paused for a few seconds and then said, "I don't know the answer to that." I looked at him somewhat surprised by his response, he didn't offer anything else. And what I discovered in that brief moment is that the genius of Ed Thorp wasn't what he knew; instead, it was his firm understanding of what he didn't know.

So often people feel the need to respond or develop an opinion about everything. Some of this is due to cultural or social habits, but a lot of it might be attributed to our own insecurities to feel smart or valuable in front of other people. The problem with the habit of always having an opinion is it's often based on superficial analysis and reason. Then as though things aren't bad enough, we develop a consistency bias toward that opinion or narrative because we want to remain consistent in the eyes of the people we are around. But if there's one thing I've learned from one of the smartest people in the world, it is this: It's not what you know that counts; it's having an understanding and appreciation for what you don't know that opens the door for intellectual opportunities in the future.

Charlie Munger has a fun quote that adds a little grit to Ed's lesson: "I never allow myself to have an opinion on anything that I don't know the other side's argument better than they do."

Lori Richardson

Lori Richardson began her career as a teacher, until becoming a single mother and needing a bigger paycheck. She knew a sales career could solve her financial challenges. She spent years as an inside sales rep, a field rep, and then a sales leader working with IBM, Apple, and HP technology products. In 2002, she launched Score More Sales, a sales consultancy that helps leaders of midsize companies solve their sales team challenges. Her latest passion is research and speaking about ways companies can hire, retain, and promote more women in sales and sales leadership—and strategies for women in sales to rise into leadership roles.

I'm twelve years old and standing on a stool while using a professional clothing steamer to steam the clothing arriving at my grandmother's women's apparel shop in Seattle. This job is my lifeline. I go to middle school and then walk to the dress shop every day after school in a North Seattle neighborhood.

We call my grandma Mimi, although her real name is Lorene Hall. I'm her "namesake," as she loves to tell everyone. In her mid-sixties, this scrappy business woman is running her third and what would be her final clothing store.

She's on her second marriage and was a single parent for quite awhile when my mom was growing up. Her income is substantial, and she's known around town because of the fashion shows she puts on and the radio advertising done with a local celebrity.

I watch her at 5:45 p.m. every day counting the money in the cash drawer, with her long, manicured nails.

Mimi doesn't discount her merchandise except during two highly publicized sales each year and has no problem selling anything at retail. She has a friendly persona and can get people to do things simply by asking. I assume it is due to a combination of her tone, demeanor, and reputation. She has a staff of women working for her, and I am learning what it is like to be a leader in her company, but there is a bigger impression she is making on me that I'm unaware of until many years later.

Three times each year is Market Week, when sales reps from New York and Los Angeles arrive representing various apparel manufacturers to show off the upcoming season's samples so stores like ours can place orders. It is nearly all salesmen who represent these companies, traveling from city to city and sometimes coming off as aggressive in pushing their wares on us.

Mimi takes no guff from these men. They show her outfits with midi-skirts and maxi-skirts. Mimi tells them that her clientele will not wear these. Unfortunately for the sellers, these skirts make up a large portion of the season's clothing, so Mimi places smaller orders.

"You're out of touch, Mrs. Hall," they say.

"You're crazy," says one in-your-face salesman.

"Go to hell!" my grandma says to him. She sticks to her guns and buys only what her customers want, later priding herself on knowing her customers better than anyone.

When the next Market Week arrives, the good salesmen apologize to her.

"You were right, Mrs. Hall."

She nods her head and knows she is.

My grandmother taught me so many valuable lessons, and the two biggest ones were:

- Know your buyer. When you know your buyer, you have a customer for life. Her customers came back to the apparel store because she always helped them look fantastic, and she pushed them to try new things when she thought they would work for them. She was honest and caring.

- Stand up for yourself. This might have been the biggest lesson for me as a youngster because it made an indelible impression on me that later helped me in dealing with strong-willed sales managers, company owners, and prospects. When I became the first woman in sales at my second tech sales position, it really came in handy that I knew I knew how to sell and knew I could bring value. I could not be intimidated, even in a climate in which other women did not survive long at that time.

Additionally, Mimi drove a hard bargain but also could be kind to someone less fortunate. I value growing up with this in my DNA.

Although many others are part of the list of those I would love to thank for helping me be the person I am today, including many who were my contemporaries, there is no contest when I think of who made the very biggest impression on me—one that's lasted all these years. Thank you, Mimi.

Michael Sadeghpour

Michael Sadeghpour is the founder of edgeThink, which offers training that bridges sports and positive psychology and applies that to the workplace. He holds a master's degree in psychology from Rensselaer Polytechnic Institute. Sadeghpour has been a competitor and a coach all his life and served as an NCAA Division I assistant men's ice hockey coach at Rensselaer. He has led several sales organizations, served on multiple executive teams, and founded ReGenerate, a positive psychology training company.

....

"Oh, East is East, and West is West, and never the twain shall meet" is a line from a Rudyard Kipling poem that I heard many times as a young man to describe my parents' budding romance as twenty-something-year-olds in the early 1960s.

My heritage, though not uncommon by today's rich melting pot of merged ethnicities created through marriage, was relatively ground-breaking at the time. My mother—a Boston-bred, Irish Catholic young woman living and teaching school in New York City—was smitten with a young Iranian visiting on leave from his job. His three-week vacation to the States was over, and an invitation to visit him in his homeland was extended and accepted by my mother.

What should have been a two-week vacation to Tehran resulted in an American life temporarily left behind and a new adventure emerging halfway across the globe, and all in the name of love. When my mother called my grandfather to share the news of her plans to remain in Iran, he uttered those famous words from the poem and added that if anyone could make that connection work, it would be her. And that she did and has, for the past fifty-six years.

Looking back on the beginning of their story, there were many memories of joy and excitement, as well as challenges. My parents were married in Iran by a Jewish rabbi in an Italian consulate because neither the Catholic church nor the mosque would sanctify their union. Where there is a will, there certainly is a way. Love will not be denied. With limited financial resources, they still enjoyed a well-lived life in an exceedingly westernized, cosmopolitan city where women were revered and honored. However, they both were anxious to start a family and were keenly aware of the limited options for male offspring.

Young Iranian men entering adulthood at that time were expected to enroll in medical school, law school, the military, or athletics, with most needing to fulfill a military requirement at some point in their lives. Uncertain of their soon-to-be newborn's talents and desires, my mother boarded a plane when she was eight months' pregnant to return to the States. I might also add this posed a tremendous challenge because she had relinquished her American passport when she wed my father. At the time, dual citizenship was not an option, and she was now considered an Iranian by her newly adopted homeland.

With some luck and a few connections, my mother boarded the plane once again as an American citizen, leaving behind her new husband. As one can imagine, this was a decision they labored over because my father's ability to leave the county was uncertain due to his remaining commitments. Her own future as a pregnant, married woman living without her husband created a state of uncertainty for both my mother and father. And although my grandfather was delighted to learn of his daughter's return home, my grandmother needed time to soothe the feelings of abandonment that were created when her oldest child headed to the Middle East.

Fortunately, my father was able to depart Iran when I was six months old. Looking back, I realize that returning to the States was the right decision for my family, given the anti-American sentiment in Iran as a result of the hostage crisis in 1979 and the war that ensued between Iran and Iraq a year later. I was seventeen at the time and would most likely have been on the front lines of a war that took over one million Iranian lives.

I have such deep gratitude to my parents for their willingness to follow their hearts and turn an unintended attraction into a love story filled with the up-and-down trials of life, regardless of cultural differences. The sacrifices they made in an effort to offer me and my sister a life filled with opportunities and choices have always been in the forefront of my own decision-making.

As cliché as this sounds, they are role models for me, both demonstrating that a little luck and a lot of hard work can result in a meaningful life filled with purpose and prosperity, however you want to define that. Although we were not a rich family, we have abundant love and appreciation for what this country afforded us. And for that, I am most blessed and grateful.

Marnie Schneider

Marnie Schneider is the founder of the Keep on Playing Foundation and author of the children's book series Football Freddie *and* Fumble the Dog. *The first book in the series,* Gameday in Philadelphia!, *was an Amazon best-seller and was inspired by her grandfather, former Philadelphia Eagles owner Leonard Tose. Her mission in life is to help others succeed by bringing sports programs to children nationwide because when kids play, we all win. She lives with her three kids, three rescue dogs, and one handsome pony.*

. . . .

I have a secret to tell you. Actually, it's more of a confession: Once a year, I get dressed up and am a little unfaithful to my true love. Facebook would kindly post an "it's complicated" status, and this is no joke. It really is complicated! I've kept this hidden for years, with only a few candid selfies carefully tucked away on my phone. Photos are all I have to show for it. But it's time to download the facts and own it.

We were in the Lone Star State. I was in my preteens with a mouth full of hideous braces, still sporting my baby fat, and proudly wearing a kelly/Eagles-green sweater dress—it was the 1980s after all. Little did I know that when the out-of-bounds person entered my life, our connection would wind up having a lifelong impact on me. It was a game-changing moment, a standing O moment.

There I was, sitting in the visiting owner's box, a heaping plate of barbecued ribs on my lap (OK, maybe it wasn't baby fat after all), sobbing hysterically over another heartbreaking Eagles loss when a stunning platinum blonde outfitted in that amazing eye-catching sparkly uniform and a warm smile approached me. Leave it to the Dallas Cowboys to position their cheerleaders in the owners' boxes! Miss Dallas Cowboys Cheerleader, who had been watching the game with us and cheering along, leaned in and whispered in my ear, with her full-on southern drawl, "Sweet girl, when I was your age, my granny taught me this. Follow her advice, and you'll see—the stars of the universe will always shine on you." It's no coincidence that the Cowboys' logo is a bright blue star.

"Be your own head cheerleader," she said. "And every year, you have to work hard to make the squad. Grab your pom-poms and get out there. Promise me you'll always go the distance to be there for yourself and others. We have a saying around here: 'There are no traffic jams along the extra mile.'" (That's a direct quote from Roger Staubach.)

I agreed, and she hugged me and was gone. I was mesmerized and committed to following her granny's advice. I'm a huge fan of those Dallas Cowboys cheerleaders.

Some kids decide they want to be a doctor after seeing their pediatrician give a shot painlessly or a policeman or lawyer after watching Law and Order. My role model was a Dallas Cowboys cheerleader. It was then that I knew my calling. Cheering for others is a skill and can make you a leader—a CHEERLEADER!

The value and importance of cheering is deep. Cheerleaders make the world a better place. It's an outstanding support system that connects you to the crowd. It's a thrill to cheer and be cheered for. We all need an advocate to encourage us. I believe that's what makes a true leader—being able to cheer for others. I love being a cheerleader for those I care about and even people I don't know who are helping others and doing good. Cheering is a strong currency.

Take a page out of the Joe Namath playbook and proclaim that you're going to win on Sunday—then guarantee it by cheering yourself to the win. I love Joe Namath. He's a leader and a legend with confidence. He owns it. Like he says: "When you have confidence, you can have a lot of fun. And when you have fun, you can do amazing things."

Sixteen years ago, my son was diagnosed with neuroblastoma, an often life-threatening type of cancer that affects young children. As a mom, I can chew glass and think it's OK, but when my baby even has a hangnail, it hurts. This was major, and I knew I had better be prepared for the worst. My innate cheering skills were at the max. I was ready, but any extra reinforcements were always welcome. I was living in Los Angeles at the time, and as I was driving up La Cienega Boulevard after a rough day for my son at Cedars-Sinai, our local hospital, I noticed a mannequin that was a perfect replica of my sparkly Dallas Cowboys cheerleader. I parked my car and immediately entered this kingdom of costumes.

I was a rookie in this boutique, and I quickly learned you have to be a member to enter. I paid my $1 dues, and after some cheering on by the women who worked there, I was suited up to play. I felt weird, like I was cheating on my precious Birds, but it was like a superhero costume. I was ready to get on the field and kick some cancer ass.

It's more than OK to be your own cheerleader. It's OK to yell and scream and jump around and know in your heart and soul that you'll be a winner when you surround yourself with a team of cheering champions. It might be awkward at first, but it's good to feel confident and cheer for yourself.

To this day, the greatest victory I have experienced is getting my son well. Thanks to amazing doctors and nurses and a lot of cheering and praying from my family, loved ones, and strangers, he's a healthy, thriving high school junior playing football and definitely dreaming of those Dallas Cowboys cheerleaders. That's why I leave my costume locked away in my closet. Only I know where it's hidden.

So back to my yearly affair. It's my tradition and reminder to cheer for myself in my superhero costume, mostly because I use that as a way to force myself to stay in decent shape. Although, truth be told, it's harder every year to squeeze into it, and the great thing with age is wisdom so it doesn't matter. When I was young, my grandfather made me a special teenage Philadelphia Eagles cheerleader, and I got to pose for a few squad photos—that darn 1980s hair almost blocked me out of the pics. My grandfather was a great man, my cheerleader for sure. He understood that I had created a special bond with the Dallas Cowboys cheerleader from Irving. A few years back, I rescued a dog. I loved him at first sight, and once I heard his name was Irving (as in Irving, Texas, where "dem boyz" play), I knew he was sent to me by my grandfather and that cheerleader as a reminder to keep on cheering.

Being grateful for everything I have is why I cheer. I want to cheer for all the leaders out there who have cheered for me. The list is long enough to fill up a few NFL stadiums and includes my three spectacular, amazing kids, who've shown me courage and strength and made me want to be as good as they view me; my extraordinary friends—old ones and new ones; business associates who step up for me again and again and actually enjoy my often overwhelming exuberance for getting kids to read and play; a close friend of mine, a former NFL cheerleader who gave me the chance to cheer for her while she was going through her cancer treatments; all the brave veterans and military service members out there who are cheering and keeping us safe; and my outstanding parents—especially my MVP mother, who is the captain and head cheerleader for me. I am honored and humbled.

So it's complicated—and that's OK. Like the Great Man Joe says, "I am a football fan, yeah, and it feels bad to feel like you're not wanted." So that's why you always have to do your best to be great, so great that you can and want to cheer for others and for yourself, and you will skyrocket and soar like an Eagle or anything you can create. Your standing O moments happen when you cheer for others and yourself.

Keep on cheering!

Captain Todd J. Seniff

Captain Todd J. Seniff is a U.S. Navy SEAL with 30 years of experience leading special operations forces in the relentless pursuit of those who would threaten our national security.

Each time we go out on an operation, the enemy gets a vote. Each time we train for war, there is a good chance Murphy will show up. Such are the risks of my chosen profession, acknowledged and accepted with a clear conscience and more than a little enthusiasm. But this is my chosen profession, not my family's.

And so with a tip of my cap, a sincere standing ovation, and an emotional "thank you" best delivered on bended knee, I wish to recognize and thank those behind the scenes who provide comfort and support and allow the warriors to go forth: the military family.

As with most of America, my wife and I watched the events of September 11, 2001, unfold with horror. As the brave first responders dug through the pile of toxic rubble in lower Manhattan, the United Airlines Flight 93 debris field near Shanksville, Pennsylvania, and the caved-in west side of the Pentagon, my teammates and I were planning and preparing to be first responders of another sort. We were going after the root cause of the issue, and intelligence indicated that the mastermind of the attacks was in Afghanistan.

To be at the very sharpest tip of the nation's sword of vengeance was a heady experience. Our cause was justified and promoted enthusiastically by every demographic in the country, and for an odd moment, there was a unified political will bent on thrusting that sword deep into the heart of any country in the world that might provide our enemy safe haven. Our collective national blood was up, and the instrument was honed and ready.

Thrust the sword we did. And we continue to thrust the sword today, with seventeen years of sustained combat as of this writing. It is what is known as a low-intensity conflict, as opposed to a large-scale set-piece war, but it is a war nonetheless, with young Americans coming back in caskets all the time. It is very real, with much at stake, despite the fact that most of our populace has lost interest by now and gone on with their interests and lives.

Back on that fateful day, however, it was beginning to dawn on us that the events of 9/11 were indeed coordinated attacks on our homeland, which meant that those in the profession of arms had reached the moment of their destiny. My wife, taking it all in immediately, bravely and without hesitation pushed me out the door and told me to do whatever needed to be done. She then, without missing a beat, gave our two baby boys breakfast.

For those who wear the cloth of our nation, time away from family is often counted in years. Yet we reward those who go forward with medals, a "thank you for your service," and health care for life. It is those who wait, however—those who keep the fabric of the family and community together, those children who have to mature perhaps a little too early, and those harried now-single parents who are on duty 24/7 running from one life task to another—who deserve the recognition. They also serve. They should get the pat on the back and a "thank you for shouldering the load."

After all, it is they for whom we fight. The need to provide security for one's family and to protect hearth and home is hardwired into animals. Never get between a mother and her cubs. And when the unthinkable happens—when the warrior comes home on his shield instead of carrying it—the family's arc of existence is forever altered.

In Steven Pressfield's book *Gates of Fire*, King Leonidas of Sparta articulates perfectly the time-honored essence of the strength of the military spouse: "Why have I nominated you, lady, to bear up beneath this most terrible of trials...? Because you can."

Because they can.

They do indeed bear up stoically under the stress, strain, worry, and anguish. Like the wives of the 300 Spartans who died at Thermopylae, they serve as an example for us all.

I stand in utter admiration for these families and from the bottom of my soul give them the ovation they deserve. Because they will never even think of it, let alone ask for it. They just carry on, with dignity and purpose. They just...do.

Kevin Singleton

For more than thirty years, Kevin Singleton has been inspiring students to make a difference on their campuses and in their communities. He has spoken to over 3 million young people in twenty countries. His basketball skills, musical talent, and motivational speaking produce an entertaining combination that holds students' attention and challenges them to make the right choices. In 2009, he founded Elevate New York, an educational mentoring program in the Bronx, New York.

....

My standing O goes to my mother, Lynetta Mouton. While I was growing up, she was known as Ms. Singleton, a famous Lafayette, Louisiana, award-winning choral director. Someone who never met a stranger out in public. President of the local Music Teachers Association for many years. A leader of the graduate chapter of her sorority. Director of children's choirs at our church. An entrepreneur who sold Home Interiors and Gifts during the week to help make ends meet and absolutely the loudest person in the gym at all my basketball games.

She began to step away from many of her civic responsibilities when I was about twelve years old and repeatedly told me this: "Bum, twenty years from now, it won't matter how many organizations I was involved in. What will matter is the kind of mother I was. I can do those things again later." I remember those conversations as though they happened yesterday, and she was right.

My father was a great man but didn't have the ability to sustain relationships. My mom and he divorced before I was two years old. Shortly afterward, my dad enrolled at Harvard Business School and graduated with an MBA in 1971. That tells you the type of pioneer he was, to be a black man at Harvard in the late 1960s. He remarried and divorced again after that.

When I was old enough to learn about my father's infidelity and connect the dots on why I only saw him twice a year in my youth, I became very angry. A Harvard MBA left us alone to struggle in the racist South on my mother's teaching salary while he worked for and purchased successful companies, became a beloved college professor, and built a separate life for himself in Texas and California.

One day I realized something profound. My mother had never said one negative word about my father. She only highlighted the positive traits about him as I grew up and began to display those same traits. Something was wrong with this picture. I wanted to cuss him out and give him a piece of my mind, but the person who was initially the most wounded and embarrassed by my dad's behavior had modeled forgiveness all my life. He certainly didn't deserve forgiveness, but that's exactly what my mom extended to him.

I'm an educator and an etymologist. When you break up and study the word "forgive," it's very powerful. The uses of "for" as a prefix are: before, in front of, and toward. The word "give" means: bestow, deliver to another, allot, grant, commit, devote, and entrust.

Wait! So, before my dad apologized (which never happened) and before he taught me what he had learned about sports, business, and finance (which never happened), my mom honored him as though he had already done those things. Where does a person acquire the ability to function this way? Why would a person function this way?

The answer is faith. My mom has always been a woman of faith, and the very essence of faith is the ability to see things before they happen or before others see them.

Because of her faith and the forgiveness she modeled, this story ends well. Following my mom's example, I called my dad when I was twenty-four years old and told him that I forgave him for everything. It was a weird conversation because he didn't know how to respond and I didn't demand a response. We hung up after an awkward silence and after saying something manly like, "Uhhh, talk later, bye."

For the next nineteen years, until he passed away in October 2007, I made it my mission to reach out to him periodically by phone, in person, or whenever I traveled to Los Angeles. I made a decision to honor him for being my father, as my mom had modeled all my life. Unbeknownst to me, he had written me into his estate plan. Honestly, in 2007, I didn't even know what an estate plan was. The money from that trust fund was the seed capital that allowed me to research and found Elevate New York.

To date, Elevate New York has raised and invested more than $2.3 million into Congressional District 16 in the Bronx, the poorest district in the U.S. Since our inception, 98 percent of the high school students in our program have graduated and more than 70 percent have pursued post-secondary education. Because of that investment, we have seen countless lives changed and have saved the U.S. taxpayers anywhere from $14.6 million to $120 million.

In the past four years, we've taken a group of students to Harvard for the Latina Empowerment and Development Conference. I tell the students every year that the journey to Harvard is special for me. My dad walked these grounds in the late 1960s and early 1970s and was distant for decades, but we were reunited through the power of forgiveness, he was generous in his final days, and the program they are benefitting from was started because of the financial principles he learned while on this very campus. It's a powerful reality in my life and in theirs.

Just think: If not for the miracle of forgiveness, would our students have had those and countless other opportunities and exposure to greatness? Scott MacGregor, the curator of this book, is chairman of Elevate New York's board. If not for the power of forgiveness, would you even be reading this book?

Thanks, Mom, Miss Netty, Netty Girl. There's no one else like you! You get my standing O for mentoring me in forgiveness.

Brandon Steiner

Brandon Steiner is founder and chairman of Steiner Sports Marketing and Memorabilia. He's a regular on ESPN New York Radio 98.7 FM and host of the Emmy-nominated The Hook-Up with Brandon Steiner *on YES Network. He appears frequently on CNBC, CNN, MSNBC, and ESPN and in* The New York Times, The Wall Street Journal, *and others. He is the author of* The Business Playbook: Leadership Lessons From the World of Sports *and* You Gotta Have Balls: How a Kid From Brooklyn Started From Scratch, Bought Yankee Stadium, and Created a Sports Empire.

. . . .

One is never enough, so although I was asked to talk about one key lesson that I carry with me, I just have to give you more. You can't say, "I have one thing to talk to you about." It just doesn't seem like one is enough, right?

And three—don't even get me started on three! Three is way too many. "Can you please do these three things for me?" Nope, doesn't work.

Two is the right number, don't you think?

Think about it: The two most important books in your life are:
1. Your date book
2. Your checkbook

That should give you some perspective on where you spend your time and where you spend your money.

The two most important days of your life:
1. The day you were born
2. The day you figured out why you were born (what's your purpose?)

There are just two things I know for sure:

1. You can plan for what's about to happen, or
2. You can deal with what just happened.

Two food rules:
1. Don't eat ballpark food before the fifth inning.
2. Don't eat sushi on a Sunday.

Don't make important decisions when:
1. You're drunk.
2. You're angry.

No matter how flat a pancake is, it always has two sides.

The two most important things in a relationship:
1. Trust
2. Communication

You don't always get what you want, but:
1. You get what you negotiate.
2. You get what you commit to.

You can't have:
1. Fear and faith at the same time.
2. A positive and a negative at the same time.

The two most important things in an employment review:
1. What I want you to do more of.
2. What I want you to do less of.

When you get out of college, you should ask:
1. What am I going to do?
2. More important, what kind of person am I going to be?

Two is the magic number. That's why in my daily life and with my employees at Steiner Sports, we count by twos.

So here are my two lessons from two influential people in my life for whom I will be forever grateful.

Jim Beard is the guy who gave me what was my dream job out of college as a management trainee in the employee cafeteria at the Hyatt hotel in Baltimore, Maryland. At the time, Jim was my food and beverage manager, but he eventually went on to become general manager of the hotel and then was a corporate executive for Regent Hotels and Resorts, ZipRealty Inc., and Wyndham Hotels and Resorts. The guy is a legend in the hospitality industry.

All I wanted was to work for Hyatt. It was a great hotel chain, and it had an excellent training program. When I arrived, it wasn't long before I felt Jim's presence as an executive. He was someone I could look up to because he demanded a high quality of presentation and service. He always got the most out of his team. And the guy knew how to dress the part. There were times where he would send me home after a staff meeting to get a haircut, or if the tie I was wearing didn't match or look right, he would cut the bottom.

Jim showed me the difference between management and leadership. He also showed me the importance of a team and how all of us were better than some of us. Under his direction, anyone on the team at Hyatt was involved in every area of the hotel—from making beds to running banquets. There was no area left uncovered when help was needed. Staff meetings were short and to the point. Management parties were long and crazy. We were a group that worked hard and played hard. We always showed up for one another regardless of the time of day.

I have tried to instill everything Jim taught me all those years ago into the way I run Steiner Sports today. We try our best to create an environment where our employees can learn and also have fun, kind of like a fraternity. I owe all that to Jim.

I left Hyatt to work at the Hard Rock Café when it opened in New York City in the 1980s. That's where another lesson comes in—from Isaac Tigrett, another one of my mentors.

In 1971, Isaac founded the first Hard Rock Café in London with Peter Morton. Ten years later, the two began to expand into the U.S. what would become a multinational restaurant empire. They split the company, and with rights to all locations east of the Mississippi, Isaac started the original New York location on 57th Street, where I became the location's first assistant general manager.

There was one particular night I recall during the opening months of the restaurant when the crowds were piling in. An average of 150 to 200 people would be waiting in a line out the door starting at 2:30 p.m. for about twelve hours, seven days a week, and this was a 250-seat restaurant with two bars!

I walked over to Isaac and said, "What do you think? It looks like we're doing pretty well here."

Isaac responded, "I'm nervous."

I didn't understand. The restaurant was off to an amazing start, yet he was in a very doom-and-gloom state at 1:30 a.m. on a busy night.

"Are we going to be able to maintain the same level of service?" he asked. "Are people going to get what they expect—and beyond—over the long haul?"

Most owners would be ecstatic about being as popular as the Hard Rock Café was in those early days, but Isaac had the long play in mind. He was worried that we wouldn't be able to meet the same quality standards as we got bigger and had more success, hired more staff, and diversified our offerings.

I was a twenty-three-year-old kid and very excited, but that night Isaac taught me something important: Real, sustained success is about not resting on your laurels and always staying hungry.

When you have a high level of short-term success, you need to look past it. The objective isn't to be popular for a little while, but to have a concept that can stick for a long time. For some people, it can be easy to get confused. But for Isaac, it was obvious in that moment that he was in it for the long haul.

Rob Thompson

Rob Thompson has twenty-five-plus years of experience as a sports marketing and media executive with the National Football League and Walt Disney Company. He is also an author and podcast host.

. . . .

I was lucky enough to have amazing mentors along my career journey, but none made as big an impact on my life both professionally and personally as Coach Tommy Groom.

I never played for Tommy; he was retired from coaching when we met. It was perfect timing because I was just starting my career and trying to figure out how it all worked, with a young family and very little business experience.

Tommy was one of those once-in-a-lifetime characters you meet, and if you read this all the way through, you will be inspired and hopefully entertained because he had some crazy stories.

His advice to me on the day we met: "Everything will fall into place, if you're headed to the right place."

Tommy grew up in a very small town in what he liked to call "West 'By God' Virginia." His blue-collar, coal-miner DNA naturally allowed him to break down life into its simplest common-sense form. He never made things overly complicated or dramatic, and he always looked for the good in people.

Tommy had a great football career at Virginia Tech in the late 1960s and then spent the next thirty-plus years coaching at the D1 level. Like most coaches, he went through a gypsy life of transitions, packing up and starting over several times and even being married several times.

The one thing I really admired about Coach was that he never seemed to miss a day of living without maximum effort, a slick grin, and most important, that infectious positive attitude.

I can remember this moment like it was yesterday. I asked him: "Out of all the places you ever coached, what was the best time in your life?"

At that moment, his brilliant response forever changed my perspective: "The best placed I've ever worked is wherever I am."

He would tell me, "Don't worry about your next job. Make sure you are taking care of the one you're currently in."

Practical advice and 100 percent true.

Coach and I traveled around the world for several years operating the National Football League's youth development programs. We put on hundreds of NFL youth events, camps, clinics, and tournaments from Boston to Bangkok, and as you can imagine, we had the experience of a lifetime. We were very lucky, and we knew it. We never took it for granted.

We worked with incredibly passionate administrators, coaches, and players from all corners of the globe. Although there were communication challenges, all of us had a shared goal of expanding a sport we loved and having the platform to make a difference in kids' lives through sports.

Tommy and I spent thousands of hours together on planes and trains, in airports and hotels, on football fields, and occasionally in some of the wackiest bars on the planet. We were invited into countless homes by our host coaches to explore their culture and spend time with them and their families.

Even though we were tired from travel and long days running events,

Tommy pushed us not to miss a chance to discover new things and build friendships that have lasted twenty-plus years.

He always said that no one really cares about how much experience you have or where you went to college; the relationships you build along the way will be the single most import aspect to your career three, five, or ten years from now.

He was spot on.

His thoughts on experience were summed up in this classic Tommy quote: "You can no more do what you don't know than come back from where you ain't never been."

Let that one sink in.

Each trip was unique and special. We discovered how small the world really is and that there are many generous, caring people in this world. That was our common connector on every stop. We heard and shared amazing stories about overcoming obstacles and how sports are a microcosm of life.

I was in a front-row seat to listen and learn from all his incredible stories and was a participant in a great deal of new ones.

But I will never forget one of the many classic Tommy moments. This particular one was in Tokyo on a promotional tour for an NFL pre-season American Bowl game.

Out of respect for our hosts, whenever Tommy addressed an audience for the first time at a press conference or event, he loved to say hello in the language of that country. He gave me the task of helping him learn the greeting on our way to the event. Sometimes I would have to remind him what country we were in, let alone teach him a second language.

I would usually spend half the flight repeating how to say hello in whatever language over and over until he could finally say his standard greeting.

Sometimes I would be left to write the phrase on napkins, but he didn't just look for my help. Typically, Tommy would include everyone around him. He would practice on the flight crew, the people on the plane, and just about everyone in the airport regardless if they were from the country we were traveling to or not.

I really do give him credit for trying, but he never got it right.

So this particular time in Tokyo, after practicing on the eleven-hour flight, we entered the press conference room, and I looked him in the eyes and had him practice one last time, which he nailed.

I'm not sure what happened in the five seconds from the time he said "Konnichiwa" to the moment he bowed, hit his head on the mic, looked at the crowd, grinned, and said in Spanish

"Feliz Navidad!"

The room went dead silent. We couldn't believe what we had just heard, and the look on everyone's face was a mix of confusion and sadness—until our Japanese interpreter respectfully broke the silence with a soft response of "Merry Christmas, Coach."

It was July.

Tommy had so many incredible stories that were out-of-this-world crazy, but as I spent more time with him, I began to understand how and, more important, why they happened.

I could listen to his stories over and over again on our travels. They never got old. The life lessons he would weave into these stories were masterful and always relevant to what he knew was troubling me or anyone else we wound up meeting on the road.

His passion was people, and he always had a way of putting challenges into perspective, whether we were in South Korea or South Carolina.

A sad but legendary Tommy story and the moment when I knew he operated at a whole different level than the rest of the world was the phone call I received from him right after New Year's in 1998.

Although it was a serious and horrible event, his positive attitude was like a slap to the head about a person's character being revealed through challenges. On January 2, 1998, the call I received from Tommy revealed who he truly was.

"Hey, my man, I have good news and bad news."

I hesitated to ask: "OK, what's the bad news?"

In a cool, deliberate voice—I kid you not—he said, "I burned my house down."

Shocked, I asked, "How did that happen?"

His response was: "Deep-frying a turkey on my back porch."

I wasn't sure if he was fooling around, but I asked, "Coach, are you and the family OK?"

"Yeah, we are all good. You know how quick I am on my feet. Got them all out safe, except for the kids' pet turtle. That thing was always too dang slow!"

We just cracked up. Somehow he had found a way to let me know it was going to be all right.

I said, "Well, if the bad news is your house burning down, what's the good news?"

Without missing a beat, he said, "We get a new house!"

He found the positive side of life during an incredibly sad situation for him and his family. They lost everything—the kids' Christmas presents, all their clothes, family photos, and thirty years of championship rings, team pictures, and other mementoes of his coaching career and life.

As time passed and he sorted out his housing and got life back in order for his family, he would tell that story with such gusto and detail that it, too, became part of his legacy. He would never allow himself or anyone around him to act like a victim in any situation and was never looking for sympathy. Instead, he turned it into a lesson for all of us.

The funny thing was he never said you shouldn't deep-fry a turkey inside a covered porch attached to your house. That part was assumed by everyone.

When someone complained to him about challenges or people, he would say, "If you can't roll with it, buy new tires."

I learned from Coach that it's all about your perspective on how to tackle the challenge you are facing—no matter how large or painful at that moment.

He would tell the person to take a second, think about it, don't get emotional, break it into common sense, and find a solution.

He loved to say this about the tough decisions: "Once you make a decision, it will be the best one you make."

He lived by the words he preached. His zest for life, football, people, and enjoying the exact moment that he was living in was contagious.

He believed that how you carried yourself was how others would perceive you. He would say, "I always have a chance to prove them right once I open my dang mouth!"

Regardless of the occasion, Coach was always the slickest-dressed person in the room. He always wore a standard sport coat, polo shirt, jeans, and cowboy boots. Out of our group of khaki- and sneaker-wearing schleps, he was the boss.

We would always tease him about his year-round tan—which you should know was only on his face. I once asked him: "Why don't you ever tan anywhere else but your face?"

In Coach's pure common sense, he said: "My man, it only matters what I look like walking in to the bar."

Another life lesson learned, Coach!

Coach Tommy Groom passed away in his sleep at the age of fifty-five in March 2003. He had been attending a coaching clinic and doing what he loved—helping and teaching others.

Coach had a major impact on all those who knew him, worked with him, and were lucky enough to be coached by him and call him a friend, dad, brother, or even ex-husband. I was incredibly fortunate to have spent all those years with him and honestly never saw him mad or heard him say a bad word about anyone.

I think of him often and the massive impact he has had on my life, especially during trying times. I only wish I had had an opportunity to say goodbye and thank him.

But I hope how I live my life by always trying my best, helping others, staying positive, and enjoying every moment is my thank you to Coach, wherever he is.

Miles Veth

Miles Veth is a vice president at SomethingNew, a nationally recognized sales recruiting firm. His responsibilities include working with business leaders to find top sales and marketing talent for their organizations and helping candidates find roles that take advantage of their strengths and interests. Veth also serves as a growth advisor to two early-stage startups, one in fundraising technology and another in data analytics. He also serves at Trinity Baptist Church and is involved in a ministry for the homeless.

....

I've read many times that a person is the average of the five people he or she spends the most time with. I have been incredibly blessed to have some amazing people who have mentored me, one of whom is Greg Swain.

Greg and I met on my second day in the sales training program at EMC, a Boston-based data storage provider (now Dell EMC). As a senior technical leader, he had been asked to give advice to my group on everything from how leaders think about information technology to how to cold-call for the first time. The minute Greg walked into the room, he controlled it with his energy in a way I had not seen before.

I quickly realized just how well he knew IT when Greg started using simplifying analogies to compare complex storage arrays to sneakers and computer networking to highway lanes. This was the first lesson he immediately taught me: Know your craft so well that you can explain it simply in a way a stranger can understand.

As the training progressed, Greg explained how competitive the 2015 IT industry had become and warned of the dangers of failing to differentiate as a sales professional in a sea of competition. He let us know that the way to win in our careers was to "stay out of the middle," instead doing everything possible to "come at things sideways." At the time, I didn't fully understand his advice, but six months later, with his guidance, we were able to crack an appointment at one of the largest Fortune 500 underpens of EMC in the world by employing a "sideways" approach. You could say I am now a big believer!

Following our first interaction, I reached out to Greg for his advice one-on-one, realizing that he had many other responsibilities but hoping he could spare a few minutes for me. That first interaction turned into endless early mornings, late nights, coffees, and lunches where Greg carefully molded me from an inexperienced rookie into someone who could take pride in what he did.

But Greg didn't stop at just giving advice; he continually encouraged me to bring him real-world situations to discuss together and made himself available to me anytime I needed him. Given his numerous other responsibilities, it amazed me how willing he was to help me when it had nothing to do with his job description and I offered nothing in return. Even after I moved on from Dell EMC, Greg's support of me has not diminished. I can't remember a single time when he hasn't returned my call. This has burned in my mind another very important lesson: Selflessly give of your time and talent to others, without any expectation of anything in return.

As my career at EMC progressed and I joined a large sales organization, I was exposed to many business leaders on a daily basis. I quickly realized there are two types of leaders in the world: those who lead from the front and those who lead from the back. Greg always leads from the front. Due to the fact that he knows the intersection of sales, technology, and business better than anyone, nobody ever questions his position of authority. Additionally, his ability to "win in the trenches" not only greatly inspires those under him, but gives him a significant advantage when thinking about higher-level strategy. I will never forget this lesson: Lead from the absolute front, and never forget how to win in the trenches.

Greg, thank you for the incredible impact you have had on my life. You've taught me positivity in a way that nobody else has, and you're one of the first people I call when I need inspiration. Thank you for taking the time to encourage me and for seeing the potential in me before I saw it in myself. Thank you for teaching me the importance of serving family first and for always having the backs of those who are close to you (me included). Thank you for showing me what true dedication to a craft looks like and for letting me see the benefits of what happens when this work is put in. Thank you for also teaching me to smile and always seeing the fun in life. And finally, thank you for teaching me humility.

You are one of the people I most admire, and I'm not sure even you realize just how much of a difference you've made in my life and the lives of others.

What are you grateful for?

Who in your life deserves a standing O?
Don't let time slip by, let them know today!

About Keep on Playing: (keeponplaying.org)

Keep On Playing enriches the lives of our youth through playing baseball. When kids keep on playing, they develop character, confidence, leadership skills, grow into lifelong fans, and have fun.

Keep On Playing builds confidence, increases motivation, enhances self-esteem, jump starts participation in sports, builds teamwork, fosters learning, produces leaders, and opens the door for youths to be part of positive opportunities.

About Elevate New York: (elevatenewyork.org)

Elevate New York builds long-term, life-changing relationships with urban youth in the South Bronx through four program areas: Accredited Classes, Mentoring, Adventure, and College and Career. Full-time, salaried teacher-mentors teach accredited, elective classes at public schools on character qualities and life skills and also mentor students outside of the classroom year-round. The students are introduced to new opportunities and experiences, equipping them with a plan for their future. Elevate New York is on a quest to build the next generation of urban leaders.